PEWTER
*A celebration
of the craft
1200-1700*

Published by the Museum of London
London Wall, EC2
1989

ISBN 0 904818 36 5

British Library Cataloguing in Publication Data
Hornsby, Peter,
    Pewter: a celebration of the craft
    1200–1700
    1. British pewterware. 1200–1700
    I. Title   II. Weinstein, Rosemary I.
    III. Homer, Ronald F.   IIII. Museum of
    London
    739′.533′0941

    ISBN 0–904818–36–5

Designed and produced by
Historical Publications Ltd
32 Ellington Street, N7

Typeset by Historical Publications Ltd and
Fakenham Photosetting Ltd
Origination by Tigeraphics Ltd
Printed in Great Britain by Printpoint Ltd

PEWTER
A celebration of the craft
1200-1700

PETER R.G. HORNSBY
ROSEMARY WEINSTEIN
RONALD F. HOMER

The Museum of London
May 1989–May 1990

Contents

Acknowledgements

The Museum of London owes a very substantial debt to the anonymous collector and is grateful for his support of the exhibition. The Museum would like to thank especially Mr Peter Hornsby for his considerable assistance in the preparation of the exhibition and catalogue; also Dr. Ronald Homer and Vanessa Brett for their help in compiling the catalogue. The Museum is grateful to Mrs Rosemary Weinstein for co-ordinating work within the Museum and colleagues John Clark and Peter Stott for providing information and advice; also Neil Stratford and Tim Wilson (British Museum), Charles Hull (The Worshipful Company of Pewterers), Ken Target of James Yates Pewter and Michael B. Green who designed the exhibition. Colour photography is by Torla Evans. We would also like to thank the following, who have generously loaned items to the exhibition:

British Museum 7, 106, 123; City Museum and Art Gallery, Birmingham, 136; the Earl of Bradford 15; Chertsey Museum 137; Christchurch Cathedral, Oxford 113, 138; Guildhall Library 1–6; Mr. Frank Holt 81, 127, 145; Jewish Museum 150; Ludlow Museum 134; Mary Rose Trust 100; Private collections 12, 14, 19, 25, 38, 39, 67, 73e, 82, 83, 104, 108; the principal private collection 11, 17a–b, 20, 27, 29–31, 33c–f, 34b–f, 36, 37, 39, 40, 43–8, 51–53, 55–58, 60–66, 72, 73a,f, 74–75, 78, 80, 92–93, 95, 98–99, 102–103, 105, 112, 115–117, 119–122, 124–125, 128–132, 135, 143–144, 146, 149; the Worshipful Company of Pewterers 13, 42, 49–50, 54, 59, 76–77, 79, 90, 97, 109, 111, 114, 118, 126, 133, 147–148. Remaining exhibits are from the Museum's collection.

THE RIGHT HONOURABLE THE LORD MAYOR
SIR CHRISTOPHER COLLETT GBE MA DSc

The Museum of London has, during its relatively short existence within our City Walls, established an enviable reputation for imaginative and meticulously researched exhibitions dealing with aspects of London life and its antiquities.

I am delighted that during this 800th anniversary year of the establishment of London's Mayoralty the Museum should, with the assistance of the ancient and Worshipful Company of Pewterers, as well as The Pewter Society, add such a fascinating touchmark to our programme of events.

My warm congratulations go to all those who have played a part in the staging of this exhibition, and my special thanks go to the anonymous private collector whose generosity has made the project possible.

Sir Christopher Collett GBE MA DSc
LORD MAYOR

THE WORSHIPFUL COMPANY
OF PEWTERERS

There is no record of the origin of the Worshipful Company of Pewterers but it is likely to have been in the early years of the 14th century, for the first documented reference to the 'goodfolk, makers of vessels of pewter' is dated 1348. The guild, with its control of craftsmen within the City, developed over the following years and by its first charter granted by Edward IV in 1474 was given authority to maintain the quality of pewterware throughout England. The growth of the trade reflected its use for both church and domestic purposes; in the mid-17th century there were over 300 shopkeepers and master pewterers within the City itself, employing as many journeymen and apprentices. Following the Industrial Revolution, with the introduction of new manufacturing techniques and other materials suitable for domestic use, the 18th century saw the start of a decline in the trade. However, today the Company is active in its support for the contemporary pewter industry: in this country represented by the Association of British Pewter Craftsmen and on the continent by the European Pewter Union. Thus for about half the period since the mayoralty was established pewterers have played a significant part in the manufacturing industry of London.

In this year of especial commemoration of the Mayoralty, it is perhaps fitting that the Museum of London should mount this major exhibition of pewter which had so important a place in the life of the community spanning four centuries. I hope that the appeal of the pieces on display, not only to the eye of the beholder but also to the hand of the craftsman who works with metals, will re-create an interest in pewter, for I am concerned that our heritage should be appreciated by as many people as possible, so that we do not allow antique pewter to be lost or destroyed through lack of awareness of its historical importance.

J.S. Holden
MASTER

Introduction

This is an exhibition of English pewter made in the period 1200 to 1700. London was the leading centre of pewter manufacture in England and the exhibition concentrates on items made in London or on forms which were used or originated in the city. Specifically provincial pewter, pewter from Scotland and that made for the Channel Islands, is excluded.

Pewter has been made in Britain from Roman times and is still being produced today. From the later Middle Ages onwards pewter was as familiar a material as plastic, steel and aluminium are today. By the 16th century it was to be found in at least half the homes in England, at all social levels. The nobility, rich merchants and prelates would have owned scores or hundreds of pieces, but the ordinary men and women who laboured in the fields and towns also ate from pewter bowls or plates, using a simple pewter spoon. The use of pewter went beyond the home, and it would have been found in church, monastery, chapel, synagogue and hospice, as well as in colleges, universities, guilds and palaces.

Pewter is an alloy of tin with other metals, such as lead and copper, which make it more durable than pure tin.

Pewter reached the height of its popularity around 1700 and then declined in the face of competition from other materials such as pottery, porcelain, brass, copper and, finally, silver plate. Nevertheless it remained in extensive use throughout the 18th century and was still being produced, especially for taverns and public houses, into the late 19th century. Interest in pewter revived briefly in the Art Nouveau period and many pieces of hammered pewter from the 1930s can still be found.

This catalogue examines in some detail the history of the Worshipful Company of Pewterers, the way pewter was produced, how it was marketed and how it was used. Its contents shed new light upon aspects of medieval and later pewter and it includes recent discoveries as well as further documentary evidence concerning the origins of the craft in London.

Previous exhibitions of pewter in this country were held in 1904 and 1908 (Clifford's Inn, London), 1962 (Lincoln) and 1969 (Reading) but until now it has not received the attention to which it is entitled.

Fig. 1. Summons to Quarter Day, 10 August 1719, at Pewterers' Hall. *(Trustees of the British Museum)*

The Pewterers of London

The ancient Livery Companies of the City of London trace their histories back to the medieval craft guilds. Their earlier undocumented origins are to be found in quasi-religious fraternities which brought together people with common interests for their mutual material and spiritual wellbeing. The Worshipful Company of Pewterers stems from one such fraternity, that of the Assumption of the Blessed Virgin Mary.

As individual crafts developed in importance their organisation became formalised within the medieval concept of collective rights and responsibilities. In return for privileges granted, originally by the City and later by the Crown, the crafts pledged themselves to maintain the quality of their products and to ensure that these were sold at equitable prices having regard to the cost of materials and labour. The simple medieval concepts of the 'just return' to the craftsman and the 'just price' to the consumer were, however, soon overlaid with increasingly complex and restrictive rules and regulations as each trade sought to enhance and enlarge its monopoly position.

The pewterers successfully petitioned the City authorities in 1348 for the grant of 'ordinances', the rules by which they would conduct their business, and as the use of pewter grew in the 15th century, they turned their thoughts to increasing their influence by seeking a royal charter. After much lobbying and expenditure by the craft this was eventually granted by Edward IV on 20th January 1473/4. It gave the pewterers the standing and privileges of a Livery Company with power to control the quality of metal and of workmanship throughout the whole country. The Company's charter was confirmed and renewed by subsequent monarchs, lastly by Queen Anne.

Today the Worshipful Company of Pewterers continues to discharge its ancient responsibilities by its sponsorship of the Association of British Pewter Craftsmen and by supporting research and education relating to pewter.

In the last decade of the 12th century Alexander le calicer (the chalice-maker) made pewter chalices in his shop 'within Ludgate towards Baynard's Castle'. He is the earliest recorded pewter chalice maker in London and one of a close-knit group of craftsmen who for long plied their trade in the Ludgate area.[1] They supplied chalices, and very likely other church vessels and furnishings, for the ecclesiastical market.

It is from these early beginnings that the 'craft' or 'mistery' of pewterers of the City of London grew to become an officially recognised trade guild and later a Livery Company. The guild controlled pewtering within the capital from the mid-14th century. Later, through the first of a succession of Royal Charters, it was granted powers which extended its control nationwide. By 1348, when the pewterers obtained their first ordinances from the mayor and aldermen, their trade must already have been of some importance in the capital.[2] They must also by then have had some form of corporate organisation capable of implementing the rules and working practices laid down in the ordinances. What then was the reason for the appearance of this coherent group of perhaps thirty pewterers[3] and their receipt of official recognition in the very year that the Black Death was to strike the city?

The realisation that pewter was a generally useful metal for which there was a domestic as well as an ecclesiastical market appears to have emerged about the end of the 13th century. Perhaps it was the result of the appearance of a class of society with money to spend on something better than the ubiquitous treen and horn, but vastly less expensive than the silver which it resembled. The evidence for the emergence of pewter as a commodity by about 1300 is threefold. Firstly, the earliest archaeological finds of pewter spoons and saucers date from c1290. Secondly, the occupational name 'le peautrer' appears by 1305; the name 'le calicer' merges with it through individuals known indifferently by both names, and eventually disappears.[4] Thirdly, records of trade in pewter-

ware and of domestic holdings of it are first found in documents from the early part of the 14th century. Thus in 1307 a consignment of pewter pitchers, dishes and salt cellars weighing some fifty pounds was exported from London[5] and as early as 1317 Richard de Blountesham of London died possessed of twelve pewter plates, twelve dishes, eighteen salt cellars and two flagons valued at 7s.[6]

The earliest London pewterer whose career can be followed in any detail was Nicholas le peautrer de Ludgate who worked from 1324 until his death in 1347/8. He was apparently successor to the business of Henry le calicer, whose daughter he married and whose former premises he occupied.[7] His will shows that he became a prosperous tradesman with a comfortable life-style. He owned four tenements in Ludgate Street and possessed a silver cup, a dozen silver spoons and two mazer cups, which he left to his son, together with ten marks of silver, 2,000*lbs* of tin and the tools of his trade. The family business came to an abrupt end when his son died of the plague a year later, and three of Nicholas' four tenements eventually became the property of other pewterers, one of whom, John Syward, was an overseer of the 1348 ordinances. Elsewhere in London pewterers were at work before the plague in the market area of the Cheap and in Friday Street to the south. One of those in the Cheap was Stephen le Straunge, lessee of a tavern 'Le Lyonn' which had shops in front and living accommodation over it. He was another of the overseers of the ordinances, and also another plague victim.

The effect of the Black Death on the newly enfranchised craft can only have been disastrous. Not only did many pewterers, and doubtless their apprentices, succumb to it, but their market also suffered severely. The evidence suggests that the craft replenished its depleted ranks by taking in members from surrounding towns. Several came from Arlesey in Bedfordshire and others from Kent.[8] Nonetheless the wardens of the craft remained jealous of their rights. Thus in 1350 the wardens certified before the Mayor and aldermen that John de Hilton had been making substandard wares, and twenty-three pottle pots and twenty salt cellars were seized from him 'the greater part of the metal in them being lead...to the deceit of the people and the disgrace of the whole trade'.[9] By 1363, when the guilds were seeking to curry royal favour, the craft had recovered sufficiently to contribute the not inconsiderable sum of 100s towards a gift to Edward III.[10]

To safeguard their supplies of raw material the pewterers purchased tin from Cornwall on a large scale. In 1360 Nicholas Hyngestworth (*alias* Nicholas le peautrer) was in correspondence with the Black Prince, as Duke of Cornwall, offering to buy the major part of the tin produced in the county[11] and in 1364 a ship carrying some forty *tonnes* of the metal belonging to a consortium of London pewterers, was seized by the French.[12] At the end of the century a Truro-born tin merchant, John Megre, was a member of the London guild and his daughters married into prominent Cornish mining families.[13] Apparently some of those dealing in tin had their own interests rather than those of the craft in mind, for in 1444 it was ordered by the City authorities that one quarter of the tin coming into London was to be reserved for the pewterers. At the same time the craft was given a right to search all tin coming into the capital for 'great multitude of tin which is untrue and deceivable is brought into this city and here sold as dear as the best tin'.[14]

In the first half of the 15th century the number of pewterers in the capital rose from perhaps sixty to about one hundred. In the hundred years following the depression caused by the Black Death their numbers had grown about five-fold. By comparison the number of gold and silversmiths varied little during this period, dramatically illustrating the increased usage of the base metal.[15] Most of the population would have owned some pewter, the poorer ones only a spoon or two, but in the households of the wealthy there were many hundredweights of the metal; if not for their tables, then for those of their servants. Margaret Paston wrote from Norfolk to her husband in the capital in 1461 bidding him 'purvey a garnyssh or tweyn of powter vesshell, ii basanes and ii hewers and xii candlestiks, for ye have to few...'[16] In taverns too its use was widespread. In 1411 it was decreed by the mayor and aldermen that every brewer, breweress, hosteler, cook, piebaker and huckster selling ale in their houses must provide themselves with pewter pots and not use any other.[17] Even in the 14th century London-made pewter had been sold abroad in significant amounts and in the 15th century it became second only to cloth among England's manufactured exports.[18]

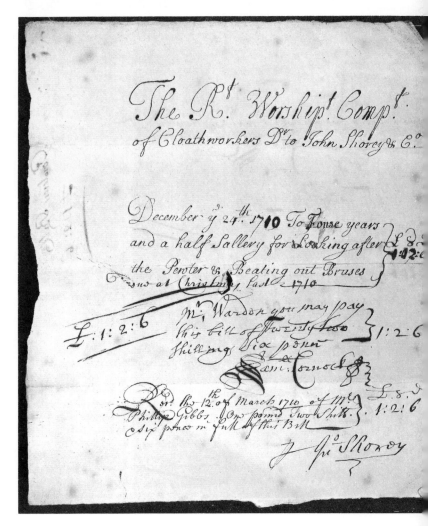

Fig. 3. Bill from John Shorey to the Worshipful Company of Clothworkers, dated 24 Dec 1710, 'To Foure years and a half Sallery for Looking after the Pewter & Beating out Bruses 1.2.6.' (*By courtesy of The Clothworkers' Company*).

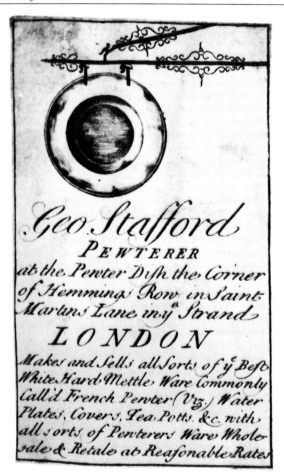

From 1427 there survives a detailed inventory of the contents of a London pewterer's workshop.[19] It was equipped with seventeen bronze moulds for casting a variety of plates and dishes from four inches to twenty inches in diameter, a lathe and turning tools, anvils, hammers, files, soldering irons, clipping shears, clamps, burnishers, bellows, casting pans, scales and weights and marking irons. Medieval pewterers' shops were small to modern eyes; in 1390 that of John Claydich, a prosperous craftsman working in Cornhill, measured only 12*ft* by 10*ft* 10*in*.[20] In the middle of the 15th century there were fifty-six pewterers' shops in the City of London.[21] Most consisted of a master pewterer and one or two apprentices or journeymen, though a few had up to a dozen craftsmen. One, exceptionally, had eighteen. By then the focus of the craft had moved from the area of St Paul's and the Cheap to the newer market areas of Candlewick Street (Cannon Street), Cornhill and Eastcheap.[22]

Newly discovered ordinances of 1455 throw much detailed light on working practices at that time.[23] Prices are laid down for a variety of wares and for workmanship. Plain vessels cost 3*d* per pound, salts 2½*d* and 3½*d* each and trenchers 3*d* each. Workmanship for making pots varied from 7*s* 6*d* to 10*s* per hundred and old metal was to be bought at no more than 2*d* per pound. Craftsmen were not to sell their wares casually in the streets, but only in their shops or at fairs. If those who bought on credit defaulted on payment, the craft was to boycott them 'of what degree that ever they be'. An interesting technical provision provides for the election to the craft of a skilled man to recover metal from the 'ashes' (dross) which formed on the melted metal and which caused significant waste of the valuable tin. The high penalty of £20 was to be paid by anyone found lending or selling their moulds out of the craft. Lastly perhaps should be mentioned the fine of 3*s* 4*d* to be imposed on any member who appeared at dinner with the mayor and sheriffs unless invited; a similar fine was to be exacted from those who were invited and did not appear!

As the pewter trade expanded in London, so pewterers multiplied elsewhere in the country. In a few major centres they were sufficiently numerous and powerful to form their own local guilds, for example in York in 1416[24] and Bristol in 1456.[25] In most cities, however, they were embraced with other metalworkers in broadly based guilds of smiths or of hammermen.[26] The competition from provincial craftsmen led the London pewterers to seek wider territorial powers to control pewtering than those given by their London based ordinances. They therefore petitioned the crown for recognition and after expending much money and effort eventually obtained their first Royal Charter in 1473/4. This gave them country-wide powers to specify the alloys to be used and to search for and seize substandard wares. The pewterers were quick to exercise these rights and embarked immediately on the provincial searches which were to be a feature of their activities until the early 18th century. Equipped with royal letters patent and hired horses the wardens of the craft made searches in 1474 in the West Country, East Anglia and the Midlands.[27] They seized much ware and cajoled or threatened some forty provincial pewterers into joining the London guild. Nearer home, in Southwark in 1478, they seized from an Ipswich pewterer suspect wares which he had just purchased in London. This turned out to be a somewhat rash action which led to protracted legal proceedings during which both the master and wardens and the supplier of the pewter were held temporarily in custody by the courts.[28]

An Act of Parliament of 1503 required all pewterers to mark their wares with a distinctive personal 'touch' so that makers of defective ware could be readily identified.[29] There is no key to these early marks, but London makers' marks from the mid-17th century onwards are recorded on five pewter touchplates still kept at Pewterers' Hall.

To meet the increasing market for pewter large numbers of apprentices were taken on until eventually there were more qualified freemen than there was work for them. In 1521 a group of unemployed journeymen petitioned the mayor and aldermen complaining of their plight in piteous terms, 'not having any goods whereby to live...nor can get any work of or among the occupation of the said craft...some of them having wife and children'.[30] The Company sought to remedy the matter by limiting apprentice numbers and in 1534 by guaranteeing employment to all those who became freemen of the craft.[31]

The Company had over two hundred members in 1600[32] and perhaps twice as many by the end of the century when the domestic use of pewter reached its peak. Throughout England the craft prospered and the search records of the Company show an energetic policing of the standards of metal and craftsmanship nationwide. Shops and fairs were visited, wares were seized, and their makers fined. The search of the Midlands in 1677 occupied the master, the wardens, the clerk and two others for over three weeks and yielded £95.13s 10d in fines. However, it showed a somewhat marginal profit of £8.18s 11½d over the expenses incurred.[33] Numerous instances are recorded of pewterers concealing their wares from the searchers or otherwise attempting to frustrate their activities. Thus in Hereford in 1640 there was a fracas at the shop of William Lee who took away the searchers' assay equipment 'and was very troublesome both in speech and deed'.[34] In London frequent searches resulted in virtually every member being fined at one time or another, and many very often, for transgressing the standards of metal or workmanship. Others were fined for buying unmarked pewterware from country makers, applying their own touch to it, and passing it off as London made.[35]

The Company also attempted to prevent foreigners engaging in the craft. They hounded a French Huguenot, James Taudin, who established himself with Cromwell's blessing in Westminster in the 1650s, forcibly entered his house in St Martin's Lane, battered his pewter with hammers and poleaxes, and conveyed it to their Hall in carts. With the Protector on his side, Taudin prevailed against the Company and they were forced to admit him as a member. After the Restoration Taudin was again harassed, but then found a powerful ally in the King. Charles II's letter to the Company (*fig 6*) bidding them to 'look on the said James Taudin as our servant' and ending 'We shall

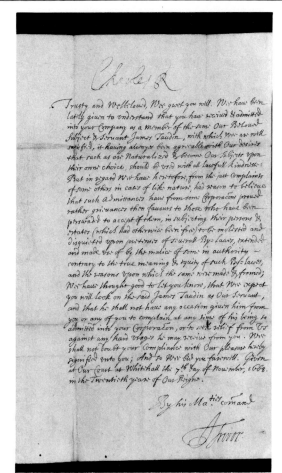

Fig. 6. Letter from Charles II to the Master, Wardens and Assistants of the Company of Pewterers, 7 Nov 1668. A transcript is given below. (Guildhall Ms 22,223). (*Guildhall Library, City of London*)

Fig. 7. (*above*) Touchmark of James Taudin. (*By courtesy of The Worshipful Company of Pewterers*)

Charles R. Trusty and Welbeloved, We greet you well. We have been lately given to understand that you have received and admitted into your Company as a member of the same our Beloved subject and servant James Taudin, with which we are well satisfied, it having always been agreeable with Our desires that such as are naturalized and become Our Subjects upon their own choice, should be used with all lawful kindness. But in regard we have heretofore, from the just complaints of some others in cases of like nature, had reason to believe that such admittance have from some Corporations proved rather grievous than favours to those who have been persuaded to accept of them, in subjecting their persons and estates (which had otherwise been free) to be molested and disquieted upon pretences of several By-laws, extended and made use of by the malice of some in authority — contrary to the true meaning and equity of such By Laws and the reasons upon which the same were made and framed. We have thought good to let you know, that We expect you will look on the said James Taudin as Our Servant and that he shall not have any occasion given him from you or any of you to complain at any time of his being so admitted into your Corporation or to seek relief from Us against any hard usages he may receive from you. We shall not doubt your Compliance with our pleasure hereby signified unto you. And so We bid you farewell. Given at Our Court at Whitehall the 7th day of November, 1668 in the Twentieth year of our Reigne. By His Maties command.

not doubt your compliance with our pleasure...' is among recently discovered papers detailing the affair.[36]

It seems likely that James Taudin was referred to as 'our servant' because he made pewter 'by appointment' to the King. Although known instances are very few it is apparent that some London pewterers were so honoured. John Stow's *Survey of London* records, in the old church of St Mildred the Virgin, the 1526 tomb of William Hurstwaight 'pewterer to the king' and as late as 1763 a London directory lists James Durand, a descendant of Taudin and a successor to his business, as 'Pewterer to His Majesty', a distinction he shared at that time with George Bacon of the Strand.[37]

Although business prospered during the 17th century, innovation in the trade was stifled. The London pewterer of the period worked within bounds which were closely proscribed by numerous ordinances and rules. Not only was the composition of his alloy stipulated by the Company, but the sizes and weights to which all types of ware had to conform were laid down from time to time in so-called 'sizings'.[38] The Company also from time to time sought to fix the wholesale and retail prices at which wares were sold and the discounts which were to be allowed to 'country chapmen' who sold them in the provinces. Rules of 1639 setting out prices and permitted profit margins even supply the argument to be used with customers who attempted to bargain.[39] 'No man shall say to a customer that he will abate him 2 pence or 3 pence or more whereby to get custom, neither shall he say that it is so ordered and therefore he cannot do it, but being metal it grows dear and wastes much therefore he cannot afford it.' Appended to the rules are the signatures of some 120 pewterers who undertook to be bound by them.

The Great Fire of 1666 destroyed the Company's medieval hall in Lime Street and doubtless the homes and workshops of many of the capital's pewterers. Its impact on the trade seems, however, to have been transient. The hall was rebuilt, and in

Fig. 8. Trade Card of Edward Quick (free 1735). *(Trustees of the British Museum)*

September 1668 it was sufficiently complete for the Company to resume holding its Court meetings there. In the following year a church service was held to give thanks to God for 'restoring the Company to almost all their estates which they had before the late dreadful fire.'[40] From the half century or so following the Great Fire come some of the finest surviving examples of London-made pewterware. The workmanship is faultless and the designs are practical and restrained. Virtually everything which could be bought in silver could also be purchased in pewter. In addition the base metal provided a range of tavern measures and drinking pots which had no precious metal counterparts. With an estimated thirty thousand *tons* of pewterware in use country-wide at the end of the 17th century the future for the craft must have seemed assured.[41]

However, despite this 17th century prosperity the writing was already on the wall. Tinplate began to compete with pewter and as early as 1666 the pewterers petitioned against the incorporation of the tinplate workers whose metal 'is not so wholesome or lasting for use as pewter, it being upon the least breach or hole in any pot or vessel rendered useless and worth nothing'.[42] But their battle was a losing one and during the 18th century pewter, save for tavern wares, was increasingly displaced by tinplate and cheap pottery and glass. The consumer's acceptance of these less durable alternatives, which could not be traded in for recasting when worn out or broken, perhaps marks the beginning of the throw-away society! Nevertheless much domestic pewter continued to be made during the 18th century and the pewterers found new markets opening up in the American and African colonies.

The influence of the Company in the country at large withered as the traditional guild system collapsed in the face of the industrial revolution. In London it maintained at least nominal control until the end of the 18th century, but by then had little real power. Pewtermaking had become an industry in which the new industrial cities such as Birmingham vied with London in supplying beermugs, measures and pewter hardware to innumerable public houses and similar institutions: a trade which died only within living memory.

Dr. R.F. HOMER
Archivist, The Worshipful Company of Pewterers

Edward Quick
Pewterer, in Lamb Street, Spittle-Fields.
LONDON.
Makes & Sells all sorts of Superfine Hard Mettle Pewter, Wholesale and Retail at ye lowest Prices.

Pewter Manufacture

Tin is the principal metal used in pewter. Tin is relatively soft and lacks strength, but with the addition of small amounts of other elements it is durable enough to withstand the vicissitudes of daily domestic life. Only in this country did a special word for pewter emerge: elsewhere the alloy is called tin, although the word employed naturally varies from language to language.

Pewter is thus an alloy of tin with other metals; the formulae used gradually evolved. Some Roman pewter contained up to 60% lead, but from the 15th century the level of lead found is seldom above 25% and commonly below 10%. The other important addition was copper. There is some confusion over how much copper could be added successfully and in practice it appears that pewter with above 10% copper is rare and that the more usual quality was about 3%. Antimony was used in Europe before 1600 but did not reach this country until the late 17th century, whilst small amounts of bismuth were also occasionally added.

It is no coincidence that in Britain and Europe the pewterers' guilds all eventually came to adopt similar standards for pewter. These standards were not imposed from outside but evolved out of practical experience. In most cases the top standard required above 95% of tin.[1] The standard used in Britain for first quality pewter was based on the amount of copper employed[2] and in practice it works out that between 91% and 97% of tin was incorporated.[3] The second and lower standard permitted the use of up to 16% of lead;[4] baluster measures, however, are frequently found with higher lead levels. A third standard was introduced in the Middle Ages for making trifle, that is small objects and toys, which allowed the use of old pewter as an ingredient.[5].

The London Company was authorised by its charters to supervise the quality of pewter made throughout England and Wales, but found it difficult to enforce the standards due to cost and distance. Individual pewterers were often greedy and made much sub-standard pewter, as lead was cheaper than tin. The Company sent out frequent search parties to check on the quality of the pewter used by provincial craftsmen. Their search books (the record of these journeys) throw considerable light on the trading practices and these are discussed in *Buying and Selling Pewter* (pp.21–27).

The tin used for pewter came from Devon and Cornwall, where tin mining had been undertaken since pre-Roman times. For much of the period under consideration the sale of tin was controlled by a Royal monopoly and the London Company acquired its raw material from tin farmers[6] and allocated it to its members. Provincial members bought where they could. Copper was imported from Germany or Sweden while lead was mined in several parts of Britain.

Most pewter was cast. However, in the period to 1400, some flatware (that is plates, dishes and chargers) may have been made out of hammered sheets of pewter, which is how most copper and some brass objects were shaped. Pewter was easy to cast as it has a low melting point. The hardening agents such as copper, bismuth, antimony and, to a lesser extent lead, were added to the molten tin in a large iron pot heated over a wood or charcoal fire. Only from the late 16th century was coal used as a fuel.

Early moulds were made of clay, which could only be used once, or stone, which did not last for long and were hard to make. Although used from 1400 onwards, bronze moulds were not universally employed until the 16th century. They were costly and required great skill to manufacture.[7] Iron moulds were also used, especially after Abraham Darby's improvements to cast-iron in the early 18th century. For items such as plates and dishes the moulds were simple two-part constructions, but for flagons and other holloware moulds were made in several sections. For a flagon, for example, separate moulds were needed for the lid, thumbpiece, handle, and one or more for the body depending on the complexity of the shape.[8] The mould had first to be treated with an agent to aid the release of the casting from the mould. Ochre, egg white, pumice and carbon black were all used for this purpose. It was necessary to heat the mould and the molten metal to just the right temperature

Fig. 9. Diagram showing the construction of a baluster measure

Figs. 10 & 11   Turning on a pole lathe and casting the body of a flagon, 1395. *Zwölfbruderbuch*, Mendelschen Stiftung, Nürnberg. *(Museum of London)*

for the metal to flow freely. Too hot a mould or alloy and the pewter would bubble and create air holes, too cold and it would not flow throughout the mould. Pewterers judged the temperature by experience, unaided by thermometers.

When the moulds were opened the casting inside was rough and uneven. The surplus metal had to be scraped or cut away with shears, iron pincers or rasps. The various pieces were carefully cleaned and planished to make them smooth and they were then soldered together. Such was the skill of the pewterer that, using only solder, an iron and the open fire, he could make the joints between the various parts invisible to the eye. Only by looking inside holloware can you see the joins between the sections.

The next task was to polish the surface. This was done partly by hand and partly using a lathe or wheel. Initially a simple pole lathe was employed but later an iron wheel turned by hand was used. The object for turning was held in wooden chucks and rotated. The pewterer held a steel or agate tool against the surface of the object being turned off, thus removing the imperfections.[9] When completed a new object in pewter would have shone like silver. Early wheels were driven using a pole.[10] The pole or tree branch was bent to impart pressure and the power created would drive the wheel

forward and back. After each movement the pole would be brought forward again under pressure through a foot pedal. In the 16th century lathes driven by a hand wheel evolved, termed iron wheels,[11] which were much more efficient. The London Company attempted to keep this advance hidden from their country rivals and craftsmen were forbidden to use these great wheels in the front of their shops, in contrast to earlier instructions that all work had to be done in public.[12/13] Unlike the brasiers, pewterers never made use of water power in their manufacturing process.

Flatware, in addition, was beaten with hammers to give it extra strength. Hammer marks can often be found on the surface of plates and dishes particularly around the booge — that is the section between the bottom of the plate and the rim.[14] The piece was then cleaned off and planished on the lathe. The backs of plates, dishes and chargers usually carry the marks of the lathe in the form of concentric circles where the bases were turned off.

The final task was for the pewterer to add his maker's mark or touch. Most pewterers had more than one punch including a small punch for spoons and toys and larger punches for bigger objects.[15] Each pewterer had to register his marks with the Guild on becoming a master. The mark contained the name or device of the maker and by

1630 a set of 'hallmarks', similar to those used by silversmiths, were often added. These pewterer's 'hallmarks' contain no date letter as they do in silver but are secondary maker's marks. Although the Guild or Company insisted that pewter should be marked by its maker, many items survive which do not carry such marks, a further indication that the writ of the Guild did not run universally. Not all pewter with a London mark was actually made in the city, for country members often took advantage of the high reputation of London pewter to mark their pewter falsely in this way.[16] To confuse things further, there are several examples of a son adopting his father's marks at the start of his own career.[17]

While much British pewter is plain and simple in design, there were several periods when pewter was decorated by the makers. Following European initiatives, in the 16th and early 17th centuries a fashion for cast decorated pewter developed[18] which was generally of superior workmanship and required finely crafted moulds to produce. Again in the 16th and 17th centuries some pewter, generally thought to have been of West Country origin, was decorated with various designs created by striking the surface with punches.[19] In the middle of the 17th century a form of engraving known as wrigglework became very popular, where naive designs were engraved on the surface of the piece. There was little formal engraving on pewter other than for identifying ownership, such as coats-of-arms. Several examples of decorated pewter are shown in the exhibition (*Catalogue* nos.110–135.)

Pewterers' workshops were small. Most craftsmen worked alone or employed a single journeyman. Journeymen were pewterers who had achieved the status of freeman within the Guild but who did not have the inclination or resources to set up as master pewterers. In the mid-17th century only about half of London freemen opened shops[20] and the rest worked as journeymen for other pewterers. The Guild required potential pewterers to serve a seven year apprenticeship which was paid for by the family. The young men or women were apprenticed at the age of fourteen and were in the care of the master with whom they worked and trained. About half the young people who took out apprenticeship became pewterers, the rest either died, turned to other trades or simply did not complete their training.[21] Not all master pewterers took apprentices. Masters were allowed only three trainees each at a time, although some took more contrary to the regulations. Perhaps between 50% and 75% of masters had apprentices at any one time. For example in Bristol between 1650 and 1700 twenty-four masters had apprentices at some stage, but another twenty-one did not.[22] It is difficult to speak of an average workshop as conditions varied according to the wealth of the master and where he worked. The typical larger pewterer's shop might have consisted of a master, a journeyman and one or two apprentices. Casual labour was forbidden.[23]

There was little room in such workshops for a formal division of labour. Craftsmen would have worked on every stage of the manufacture of an item, although some mundane tasks would be allocated to apprentices. However master pewterers did tend to specialise in the kind of work they produced. A few smaller pewterers would have only made spoons or trifles such as toys and buttons. Others would have concentrated on the most popular lines, which were plates, dishes and chargers; while others again would have made a wide range of objects. There is some evidence too, that a few pewterers concentrated on flagons and more complex forms.[24]

Life expectation was much less than today and it is possible to find out the average working life of a London pewterer in the 17th century, using figures for the number of shops open and the freemen enrolments. On average pewterers worked for

Fig. 14. A stock of moulds

twenty-six years, to which must be added the seven years of their apprenticeship.[25]

It was costly to set up as a pewterer, especially in London. John Hatcher recorded that it required, in the 17th century, between £300 and £1,000 to open a workshop.[26] Costs would have been lower outside London. An analysis of thirteen inventories of pewterers who died between 1660 and 1710, prepared by Homer and Hall, indicates that their estates averaged £339.[27] This includes all their possessions. It is unbalanced, however, by the inclusion of one very rich pewterer, Sampson Bourne of Worcester, worth £3,275. Excluding this one estate, the average for twenty-five pewterers between 1625 and 1700 was £154 and the median estate £136. Clearly country pewterers did not have to be as wealthy as Londoners to work in the craft. It is interesting to compare these figures with other metal trades. In one study, nailers and smiths had average estates at death of £38 and £80 respectively, whilst silversmiths and goldsmiths in London needed a capital involvement similar to pewterers to set up in business (£500 to £1,000).[28]

Apart from premises, one of the most expensive elements of starting a business was to buy moulds. Many pewterers could not afford to have many sets of moulds and they either borrowed or hired them from other members. In London the Company held a stock of moulds which it hired out. In the mid-15th century, for example, the London Company bought fifteen moulds for plates, dishes, bowls and saucers.[29] In 1521 further saucer and salt moulds were acquired[30] and in 1549 it is recorded that there were nine sadware moulds in the Hall.[31] Another example of pewterers sharing moulds comes from York where in the 17th century all new freemen had to pay the sum of

£7.10s 0d on entry towards maintaining the Guild's stock of moulds.[32] It is difficult to generalise about how many moulds pewterers owned and what was their value. Examples exist of pewterers who owned a single mould, such as Ralf Hartland of Weeks St Mary, Cornwall, who had one spoon mould at his death in 1663.[33] Other inventories record larger stocks. Richard Plummer of Ludlow (1689), for example, had 1,236*lbs* of moulds[34] whilst Thomas Gorton of Birmingham (1693) owned 1,232*lbs* of moulds. We do not know just how many moulds were included in these weights but from the inventory of another pewterer we find that twelve sadware moulds weighed an average each of 29¼*lbs*, so the stock of both of these men must have been substantial. As another example we know that Martin Williams of Bodmin (1695) owned the following number of moulds: three platter, one porringer, two tumbler, two flagon, one salt, one bleeding bowl, three spoon, and one screw, although they were only valued at £4. Six Cornish pewterers of the mid-17th century owned moulds of an average value of £15.6s 3d on their deaths, whilst three other Midlands pewterers, in a more substantial way of business, averaged £30.7s 11d.

After the moulds the next most important piece of equipment was the pewterer's wheel. Many pewterers owned one wheel only but others, including Francis Trapp of Worcester (1633) and Richard Plummer, each had three wheels.[35] From Martin Williams' inventory we learn that different wheels could be used for holloware and sadware. Many other tools were employed in the workshops.[36] These, like the wheels, were not of high value but it is interesting to record the kind of equipment pewterers employed. In many inventories there are records of pewterer's hammers.

Also found are rasps, shears, burnishers, soldering irons, clamps, vices, anvils, ladles and hucks or haucks (chucks). Tools were not expensive, as we can see from the inventory of Richard Parshouse of Worcester (1684), who although a large-scale pewterer and a wealthy man, owned a wheel and tools worth only £4.

In addition to tools pewterers needed to carry a stock of unworked metal and completed goods. Although more than fifty-five pewterers' inventories are known, only about twenty give sufficient detail for comparisons as to values of tools, stock and materials to be made and these may not be representative. Whilst they probably record accurately the number and value of moulds and tools, they may not reflect so well the levels of raw metal or finished goods for sale. Many of the dead pewterers will either have been old and inactive or sick before their death and the business may well have been run down. Still these inventories indicate substantial levels of stock in all three areas.

Some pewterers died with a substantial stock of pewter ready for sale.[37] John Trapp of Worcester (1675) owned 496*lbs* of sadware and 761*lbs* of trifle valued at £24.15*s* 1*d* while Richard Plummer had £29.10*s* 4*d* worth of worked goods at his death. Richard Williams of Saltash (1623) had £5 worth of dishes and £10 worth of holloware, whereas Peter Towsend of Liskeard (1667) had only £2.7*s*

worth of stock when he died.

In unworked metals stocks also varied considerably.[38] Typical are Joseph Seney of Walsall (1630) who had 112*lbs* of fine metal and W. Nichols of Walsall (1578) who owned 112*lbs* of alloy at their deaths. Jonathan Baron of Liskeard (1713) carried stock of over £23. Unworked metal was worth between 9*d* and 10*d* a pound at this period, so this amounted to around 550*lbs* of pewter.[39]

We can see that whilst the manufacture of pewter was generally on a small scale, there were many levels of operation. Some pewterers produced a full range of goods while others concentrated on a limited number of items. Common to all pewterers, however, was the fact that the goods they made were produced by a craftsman using simple hand tools. The way in which pewter was made changed little from the 12th to the 19th century. Only with the development of Britannia Metal (first made *c*1770 and in its heyday in the 19th century) when objects were no longer cast but spun under pressure around wooden forms, did the manufacture of pewter evolve.

The pewter created by traditional pewterers was finely worked and skilfully put together and that which survives is a monument to their craftsmanship.

P.R.G. HORNSBY

Fig. 15. Randle Holme, *An Academie of Armory,* 1688. 'The next trade is the Pewterers, whose Instruments both for Shape and Variety are not short of any, it being a Trade that requireth many Tools, because from it proceeds much invention, as also diversity of shapes.' (BL C.101.h.2) Roxburghe Club 1905. (*Guildhall Library, City of London*)

Fig. 16.   Molten metal at Englefields, East London, one of the world's oldest remaining pewter manufacturers. (*Homes and Gardens*)

Buying and Selling Pewter

Londoners would have had no difficulty in buying pewter. Pewterers were to be found throughout London and there was a steady rise in the number working there, from around fifty workshops in the late 15th century to between fifty and one hundred in the first half of the 16th century. During the latter part of the 16th century the number rose to one hundred and fifty or so and the 17th century saw a rapid rise in pewterers' shops to close on four hundred by the end of the century.[1] Pewter workshops were concentrated in Bishopsgate and Billingsgate wards with many shops in Cheapside and Cornhill, but they were also to be found in most parts of the City.

From the 15th century most large provincial towns also had pewterers at work but there were more in London than in any other town. Large cities like Bristol and York had substantial pewtering communities. York, at its peak, had around thirty master pewterers while Bristol could boast of between forty and ninety master pewterers in the 17th century.[2] Other large towns or centres such as Worcester, Gloucester, Coventry, Cambridge, Newcastle, Lincoln, Norwich and Walsall would have had ten to twelve pewterers at work by 1680.[3] Wigan was an exception: although only a small country town, more than two hundred pewterers were working there at various times in the 17th century.[4] Just why this town became a pewtering centre is not clear, but from its central position it was able to serve a wide area where other pewterers were less active and it may have benefited from the decline of the craft in York. At least another one hundred and fifty smaller towns and villages also had one or two craftsmen trading in the 17th century.[5] Many towns such as York, Bristol, Norwich, Coventry and Ludlow had a pewterers' guild and other towns like Southampton, Chester and Hereford possessed a hammermen's guild to which pewterers and other men working in metal belonged.[6] When comparing the number of pewterers at work in London and the provinces there can also be some confusion from the fact that some provincial pewterers were also country members of the London Company.[7]

Howard Cotterell identified over six thousand makers, mostly through marks on surviving pewter.[8] More recent local research has suggested that many other pewterers existed, although examples of what they made have not survived.[9] Hatcher calculates that by the end of the 17th century there were at least 1,250 master pewterers at work in the country and that with journeymen and apprentices the total numbers employed were as high as 3,500.[10]

Nevertheless pewter remained a minority trade.

For example, we know from the Gloucestershire muster rolls of 1608 that of 17,000 people whose occupations are recorded, only sixteen pewterers were named compared with 430 smiths, 54 nailers and 23 cutlers.[11] A study of Bristol apprentices between 1532 and 1542 recorded 1,449 apprenticeships entered into, of which 121 were tailors, 91 were coopers or hoopers, 71 were leatherworkers, 65 weavers, 60 tuckers, 53 cordwainers, 51 grocers, 44 smiths, 43 bakers and 41 barber-surgeons; only fifteen pewterers are listed.[12]

Not all the craftsmen offering pewter for sale in the smaller towns were active pewterers themselves. Many made only the more popular items and bought the rest of their stock from other leading regional pewterers. A few probably acted only as retailers.

As we will see in a later section of the catalogue, the demand for pewter rose steeply in the 16th and 17th centuries and by 1680 most people who were not paupers or beggars would have owned some pieces. However pewter remained a relatively costly semi-luxury for many and it was only an occasional purchase even for the wealthiest individuals. It is hard to make accurate comparisons because of the lack of statistics and because the standard of living and wages varied throughout the country. Pewter which had cost $4\frac{1}{4}d$ a pound $c1500$ rose to $9d$ a pound by 1600. In the 17th century its cost was to peak at around $1s\ 2d$ a pound $c1646$–70 but settled back to about $11d$ a pound by 1700.[13] Thus a set of twelve plates would have cost about $9s\ 8d$ in 1680. A soldier in Cromwell's army earned $8d$ a day, a casual farm labourer received around $6d$ a day whilst a skilled mason, thatcher or carpenter could earn $1s$ a day. To put this into real terms, a skilled man would have to work for perhaps ten days to earn the money to buy a dozen plates whilst a labourer might have to work for up to twenty days to make the same purchase. Another way of looking at the price of pewter is to compare its cost with that of food staples. In the middle of the 17th century beef cost $3d$ a pound, cheese $2d$, butter $6d$, bread $1\frac{1}{2}d$ and ale $1d$ a quart. One new plate would have been the equivalent of buying roughly $4lbs$ of beef or $6lbs$ of cheese, or $8lbs$ of bread or three gallons of ale. Of course there were many wealthy people in Britain and for the merchant or knight with an income of £500 a year, pewter would have been easier to buy.

If you took back old, damaged or used pewter when you needed new items, there would be a generous discount. In 1500 this could amount to half the cost of new pewter but by 1680 old pewter had risen in value to about $9d$ a pound.[14] In effect this rise in the value of old metal cut into the

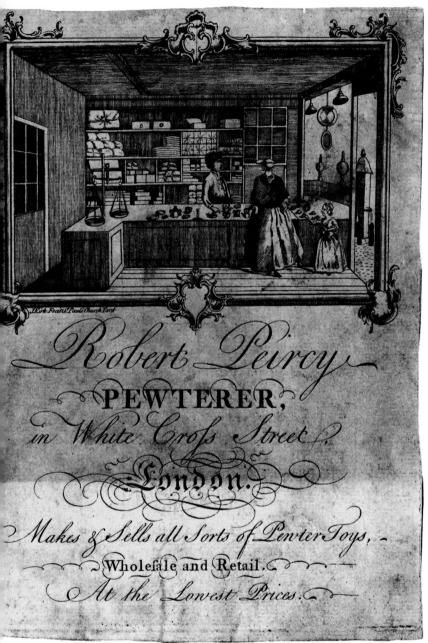

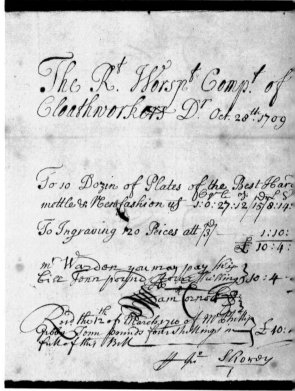

pewterer's margins. For the first time buyer, as with houses today, pewter was not cheap, but for those with old pewter to trade in the net cost was easier to afford. For example, when buying ten dozen new plates weighing 139*lbs* in 1709 the Clothworkers' Company traded in 41*lbs* of old pewter which could be re-worked.[15] (fig. 18)

Pewter was reasonably durable but its exact life expectancy is hard to calculate, as this would depend on the object itself and the way it was used. Most people would only need to buy once or twice in a decade, but institutions, where pewter received heavy use, needed more frequent purchases. Winchester College, for example, bought pewter in eight out of ten years towards the end of the 17th century.[16] The Clothworkers' Company bought twelve pewter candlesticks in 1701 only to need another twenty-four by 1715. It seems likely that, if well cared for, most domestic pewter would last ten years or so.

A large proportion of people had only limited access to shops of any kind. As late as 1700 eight out of ten people lived not in towns or villages but in the countryside. They bought and sold the necessities of life such as food, cloth, candles and ale in weekly markets. Most countrymen lived within two or three miles of one or more local markets and it is here that they went to sell their farm produce and to buy what they needed. Even in London fairs played an important role, as that held at St Bartholomew's will attest. The concept of permanent retail shops, even those selling food, was new even in the more populated areas. Within the weekly or daily markets there was a tendency for trades to group together in parts of the market. The butchers congregated in what was called the Shambles, grain was sold from the Corn Market, hay from Haymarket, sheep from Sheep Street and so on. Few towns outside London, however, had special market areas for consumer durables, although an occasional Silver Street still exists to-day in some market towns. People tended to buy these consumer durables — that is the more costly occasional capital purchases such as pewter — either from local makers, if there was one within easy reach, or from the many annual or bi-annual fairs which were held throughout Britain.

In addition to pewterers' shops in towns and booths at fairs there were many small itinerant traders who hawked pewter from street to street and from market to fair. These chapmen, hawkers or pedlars carried their stock on their back or on pack-mules. They did not have a good reputation amongst either the pewterers, from whom they obtained their stock, or the public.[17]

It would be wrong to think of a 17th century pewterer's shop as anything like a modern store. There would have been no glass display window with goods neatly presented for inspection. Pewterers sold their wares from their workshops.

These would have been busy, dirty and hot places, full of noise, with craftsmen hammering away or pouring molten metal into moulds amidst piles of tin ingots, partly completed pewter and pewter ready for sale. Eventually pewterers began to make use of their front room for retailing and kept their workshops out to the back of the premises. It is from this division that the concept of a retail shop developed.

Unfortunately we have only a slight idea to guide us as to what such pewterers' shops looked like. We have some evidence from early 18th century trade cards and from European prints and drawings. Based on what we do know, it appears that they mostly had a simple counter across the room with shelves behind and with sawdust or straw on the floor. There would have been a complete absence of advertising material and no attempt was made to present the stock attractively. Pewter dishes and plates would have been piled up on the shelves together with other popular purchases such as baluster measures, tankards, salts and candlesticks. Some pewter would be on display while other items were wrapped in rag or oiled paper parcels. In other parts of the room there would have been baskets packed with sets of plates and dishes, protected from damage with straw. Pewter being sent out of town or exported was stored for travel in wooden barrels. Shops were small: in London and most towns they were usually under eight feet wide, the whole premises extending backwards for perhaps eighteen to twenty-six feet.[18] Only later did shops gradually become larger. Outside the shop would have been a trade sign, usually a replica of the Pewterers' Arms and the name of the master craftsman would have been painted above the entrance.

London pewterers sent much of their pewter by sea to the south-east and south of England. Sea transportation was only about one-twentieth of the cost of using a horse and cart and the port record books list regular small shipments of pewter from London to such towns as Sandwich, Dover, South-ampton and other ports, small creeks and harbours.[19] In 1683, for example, 1,001 ships left London for eighty local ports. Much of this pewter went to general merchants rather than pewterers. For example, Thomas Papillion of Dover, a merchant and the local Member of Parliament, received two boxes and a barrel of pewter on the *Aventure* in October 1680 and a further shipment of 3¾cwt on the *William* in January 1681.[20] Thomas Palmer, a well-known Canterbury brass founder who made fine skillets, mortars and bells, was sent 2cwt of pewter through Sandwich in May 1671.[21]

Many of the aristocracy and rich gentry bought their pewter directly from London rather than from local craftsmen. For example, Lord de Lisle, at Calais in 1535, ordered the dishes he required from his man of business, John Husee, in London.[22] The owners of Chirk Castle, now in Clwyd, in the late 17th century bought their pewter directly from London.[23] Others, like the Edgecumbes of Cotehele in Cornwall, bought much of their pewter locally from members of the Dolbeare family at Ashburton in Devon.[24]

Pewter would also have been shipped by river and then over short distances by horse or cart. Celia Fiennes comments in her *Journal*, on seeing

Fig. 19. 'Do you want any spoons any Hard Mettle Spoons Have you any old Brass or Pewter to sell or change' etching, after Sandby, c1760. (*Museum of London*)

Fig. 20. The Pewterer's Shop, Jan & Kasper Luiken, Amsterdam, 1718. (*Guildhall Library, City of London*)

Fig. 21.   Bristol Quay, showing the shop of Richard Going, pewterer, on the extreme right-hand corner, English School, c1730. (City of Bristol Museum and Art Gallery)

long lines of packhorses in Devon. The evidence is that pewter, being heavy, was more commonly transported on land by horse and cart. In the 15th century there were regular runs between major cities; for example carts left Southampton for Winchester, London and Oxford.[25] Such journeys by cart were ninety-six times more frequent than those with pack animals. In the 16th century there were waggons with a capacity of four tons and during the 17th century larger carts were developed capable of carrying twice that weight pulled by teams of twelve horses. Carts could cover up to thirty miles a day. However, the high cost of transport, the heavy weight and relatively low value of pewter, suggests that it was seldom moved in any quantity more than one or two days' journey from its landing port or place of origin. The appalling conditions of the roads also meant that for much of the winter they were impassable.

From the search books of the Pewterers' Company[26] we have some idea of how many pewterers were operating in the towns and villages that the searchers visited in the 17th century. For example, at Salisbury in each of their three searches in 1671, 1684 and 1697, there were five pewterers in the city. Demand for pewter was still strong enough to sustain pewterers at Blandford, Dorchester, Romsey, Winchester, Chippenham and Ringwood.

Many of these local pewterers made such popular items as plates and dishes (collectively known as sadware or flatware) but bought in from other larger local pewterers those things less frequently required by their customers. If we look at the pewterers along the Great West Road (now known as the A4) in several searches between 1669 and 1693, thirty-five shops in Hungerford, Reading, Marlborough and Newbury were examined, and the work of other local pewterers found in eighteen cases. Pewter made by Cotton of Marlborough was found in the shops of Mabberley and Robinson (of Hungerford), the widow Child, Anthony Child, Susan Child and Toser (of Newbury), Biddle and Bartlett (of Marlborough) and Pidgeon (of Reading). The works of Frewin and Burgin of Reading were also frequently found in other shops along the route. In another group of towns selected at random (Tewkesbury, Devizes, Chippenham and Wrexham), the work of twenty-four other craftsmen was found in seven local shops.[27] Walsall pewter was to be found in shops over an area of 600 square miles and as far apart as Hereford in the

west and Northampton in the east, Abingdon in the south and Ashbourne in the north.[28] This was an exceptional catchment area and we do not know why. More representative of the general areas covered is that of Cotton of Marlborough whose work (already cited) was to be found over roughly 270 square miles[29] or that of Bourne of Worcester, whose coverage was restricted to about 160 square miles.[30]

Much pewter was frequently to be found in fairs, sold by local pewterers from booths or hawked round the fair by chapmen. Harrison, in the 16th century,[31] wrote that there were few towns 'that do not have one or two or more within the compass of the year'. Such fairs were held the length and breadth of the land from the earliest medieval period and many still survive today as fun fairs. Some were small, centred on a few commodities such as corn, hops, wool, cattle or horses, but many

were large, lasted several days and brought together all kinds of traders.[32] The great fairs developed their own laws, courts and market authorities. The Winchester fair, in the 16th century, lasted between sixteen and twenty-four days. By the 17th century this fair had shrunk to only eight days spread over two separate periods. Most people were within one day's walk or ride of several fairs. These local fairs lasted two or three days and were important commercially. They also provided a chance to escape from the pressures of everyday life; at the fair you could eat ginger bread, drink quarts of ale, buy a ribbon for your girl, or watch strolling players perform a mystery play or some modern drama.

From the search books of the Company we know something of the pewterers whose work was examined at fairs in the 17th century.[33] Examining the records of thirteen fairs between 1640 and

Fig. 22. A dealer in
tinware, after Christph.
Kilian, 18th century (*By
Courtesy of the Board of
Trustees, Victoria and
Albert Museum*)

Fig. 23. 'Fondeur de
Cuillers d'Etain', from *Cris
de Paris*, C. Vernet.
(*Victoria and Albert
Museum*)

1677 at Chipping Norton, Bicester, Wallingford,
Atherton, Modbury, Stourbridge, Tetbury, Wel-
lington, North Allerton, Stony Stratford, Winslow
and York, we find there are no hard-and-fast rules
about how many pewterers attended. In some
cases only one or two booths would have been
erected, whilst at others upwards of six or more
pewterers would have been present. In three cases
pewterers selling at fairs offered only their own
pewter but on average the work of between three
and four other pewterers was found in the booths.
At the Stow-on-the-Wold fair in 1682, for example,
John Carpenter had pewter from his own shop at
Burford, spoons from Oxford, porringers from
Shipston and a flagon from Coventry in his tilt or
booth.[34]

Pewterers usually made one or two days' journey, at the most, to get to a fair. At Stourbridge in
1677 two pewterers had come sixty miles from
London, but generally more modest journeys were
involved. At Blackburn in 1676 four Wigan pewterers had brought goods some nineteen miles. At
Modbury in Devon in 1641 two pewterers had
come twenty-three miles from Ashburton. The
goods they brought to sell had often originated
further afield. For example pewter from Walsall
was found at Banbury fair fifty miles away and at
Wallingford fair, seventy-five miles distant.[35] At
Stourbridge fair near Cambridge in September
1677[36] there were at least five pewterers present.
Between them they had the work of six other makers on their booths; pewter from Richard Bryden of
Cambridge was on four of them. This was one of
the most important fairs in the 17th century and
Daniel Defoe has left us a vivid account of the
event.[37] 'The shops are placed in rows like streets
...Scarce any trades are omitted...in a word all
trades that can be named in London.' Pewterers

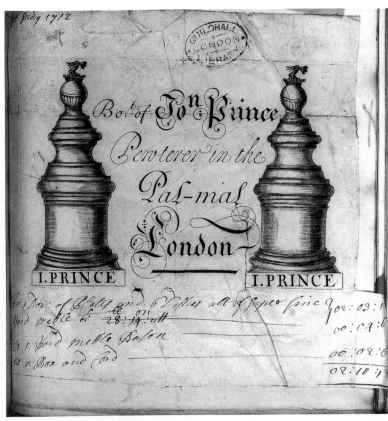

are specifically listed and in addition 'there are coffee houses, taverns, brandy-shops and eating houses...all in tents and booths'. Other sources tell us that many booths were constructed of wood, some of canvas although smaller traders would have sold from their carts or hawked their goods on foot around the fair.

We know from the lists of substandard goods found by the Company that a wide variety of pewter was available. Thomas Morton, for example, had dishes, porringers, two-eared cups, saucers, quart and half-pint wine pots and chamber pots in his booth at Stourbridge. Confirmation of the range of goods present comes from records of other fairs. At Tetbury, for example, in 1677 there were saucers, bell candlesticks, spoons, dishes, chapnetts, porringers, chamber pots, flagons, ordinary candlesticks, salts, forks and wine pots.

Mention has already been made of chapmen and hawkers, whose role John Hatcher sums up with the words 'a substantial proportion of the retail trade remained in the hands of itinerant dealers'.[38] There was a long-standing love-hate relationship between these tradesmen and the London Guild. On the one hand they were an excellent source of trade. They were often, unofficially at least, employed by members to sell pewter from door to door or in markets and fairs in the provinces,[39] and many poor pewterers resorted to hawking their goods round the country. However, chapmen were a constant source of difficulty. They undermined the operations of the Guild by repairing pewter and thus limiting the market for new wares. They also traded in old pewter, a practice condemned by the Guild as it again weakened demand for new

goods.[40] They were often unscrupulous, selling poor-grade pewter and falsifying weights. The Ordinances of 1455 outlawed selling in the streets of London and elsewhere and these restrictions were regularly re-enacted,[41] but it proved impossible to control the operation of pedlars outside London and the Guild was often forced to compromise. For example, in 1591 it actually bribed one John Backhouse to give up hawking by giving him 5s to buy tools to set up on his own behalf.[42]

On the surface it appears that the retail trade was divided into clearly defined groups: London Guild members, provincial pewterers and pedlars. But in practice, as we have seen, the groups cooperated with each other to some degree, to sell pewter in shops, at fairs and in the market place.

P.R.G.H.

Fig. 24. *(left)* Hard Metal Spoons, from *Etchings of Remarkable Beggars*, John Thomas Smith, 1815. *(Victoria and Albert Museum)*

Fig. 25. *(above)* Bill dated 1712 from John Prince of Pal Mal, London (free 1697). His touchmark is shown below *(Fig. 26)*. 'For 1 doz: of Plates and Platters all of Superfine Hard Mettle, 28lb 14oz 2:3:1½; 1 Hard Mettle Bason 4:6; A Box and Cord 2:6; total 2.10.1½. *(Guildhall Library, City of London)*

Fig. 27. Flagon, 16th century. (See *Catalogue no.41*)

Fig. 28. 'Bell' Candlestick, *c*1580–1620. (See *Catalogue no.45*)

Pewter: its development and use

For over six centuries pewterers have manufactured an endless variety of objects for domestic, ecclesiastical and other purposes in utilitarian and decorative forms. During the 16th and 17th centuries the majority of table utensils were made of this attractive metal, which replaced wood and other organic materials for these purposes, and was then itself outmoded by fashionable pottery and porcelain towards the end of the 18th century.

The several hundred or so pieces of Roman pewter found in Britain indicate a pewter industry of reasonable size in the 3rd and 4th centuries. With the departure of the Romans about 410 there is no reference to the craft for almost six hundred years, although certain ornaments that can be dated to the period appear to be made of some form of tin alloy. The most significant of such ornaments is a hoard of pewter jewellery attributed to the 11th century and found in Cheapside in the City of London. The hoard was probably the stock of a jeweller, and some of the pieces remain newly cast and unfinished (*Catalogue* no.8).

A letter from Abbot Aelfric to Wulstan, Bishop of Worcester in c1006 reveals the first known mention of English pewter. This ordered that chalices should be of fusible material, gold or silver, glass or tin (*tinen*) and not of horn or wood.[1] (The word tin would have described pewter at that time). Pewter or lead funeral chalices and patens for burial with priests were also made from the 11th to the 15th century (*Catalogue* no.11). Chalice makers worked in the parish of St Martin's Ludgate, London, from at least 1190, and in the adjoining parish of St Bride's Fleet Street.[2]

But chalices were only a fraction, albeit the most sacred, of the metal utensils of medieval churches. The earliest surviving religious object of pewter is a crucifix of the late 12th century from Ludgvan Church, Cornwall (*Catalogue* no.7). This unique Romanesque survival is significant both for its sophisticated craftsmanship and as coming from Cornwall, the source of tin. The importance of other ecclesiastical pewter is exemplified in the earliest detailed church inventory, that of St Augustine Watling Street, London, between 1160 and 1181, which records the holdings of the church as a silver-gilt chalice with silver paten, two pewter cruets, a pewter water pitcher, two copper candlesticks and two wooden and two small bowls of unspecified material.[3] Cruets, the small covered vessels used to serve the wine and water for Mass, were the most numerous pewter items in medieval churches and seem rarely to have been made of any other metal. Cruets are represented in the exhibition by those from Tong Castle, Shropshire, Weoley Castle, nr. Birmingham, and Chertsey,

Surrey (*Catalogue* nos.15, 136, 137), attributed to the 14th century. Other church pewter included pyxes (locked caskets in which the Eucharist was reserved) and chrismatories (locked containers for holy oils) (*Catalogue* no.138), censers, incense boats and their spoons, holy water vats, sprinklers, small wine barrels, font bowls and small bells.

It appears that the 14th century was the peak of consumption of ecclesiastical pewter.[4] An Italian visitor to England at the end of the 15th century remarked 'above all are their riches displayed in church treasures, for there is not a parish church in the Kingdom so mean as not to possess crucifixes, candlesticks, censers, patens, and cups of silver'.[5] Certainly inventories of the 15th century reveal some decrease in the amount of pewter held by parish churches, and the mass of mid-16th century inventories compiled to assess the value of church goods after the Reformation prior to confiscation demonstrates a substantial increase in utensils made from silver and copper alloys and a corresponding decline in those of pewter.[6]

From the 13th to the 15th centuries the pilgrimage enjoyed great popularity. Signs or badges made of lead and pewter, cast in stone or metal moulds, were sold at shrines and worn by pilgrims

Fig. 29. The Christening of Richard Beauchamp, Earl of Warwick; the cleric on the left holds a chrismatory, 15th century. (British Library, Cottonian Ms Julius E.IV). Roxburghe Club 1908. (*Guildhall Library, City of London*)

Fig. 30. Richard II dining with the Dukes of York, Gloucester and Ireland, showing trenchers and platters, 15th century. Ms Royal 14.EIVf.265v. (*By permission of the British Library*)

Fig. 31. Still Life (detail), showing plates, a salt and square trenchers of pewter, Dutch, late 16th century. (*Museum van Abbe Eindhoven. A Frequin*)

Fig. 32.   Flat-lidded Tankard *c*1670–80. (See *Catalogue no.124*)

Fig. 33 Dining at Home, using porringers and spoons, 17th century, woodcut. From *Roxburghe Ballads* (BL). (*Museum of London*)

as proof of their visits. The name 'ampoller' as a maker of pilgrims' ampullae is found in the records of Canterbury Cathedral about 1200.[7] Many of these religious souvenirs have been found in the River Thames, as have a variety of secular badges, toys, jewellery and tokens. Although the production of toys and other small objects in pewter continued to the end of our period, little pewter jewellery of 16th or 17th century date has been recorded (*Catalogue* nos. 19–26, 68, 69, 140–142).

Pewter had been used for some three centuries in religious ceremonies before it was familiar in the home. Nevertheless, the amount of religious pewter in the nine thousand or so churches, abbeys and cathedrals of the country was probably tiny by comparison with the amount of domestic pewter by the end of the 14th century.

Between 1292 and 1298 lists of stores in Berwick Castle include two pewter cruets for use in the chapel, a pewter basin, and pitchers of tin and pewter in the larder. Unfortunately none of these pieces survive and we can only speculate on their country of origin.[8] Apart from this reference we have no evidence of pewter in domestic use in aristocratic households in the 13th century. Records for royal households show the difference in cost between utilitarian pottery vessels and pewter. In 1290, for example, 100 pottery dishes, 100 platters and 124 salt cellars were purchased for Edward I at a cost of 7*d*, 14*d* and 4*d* respectively,[9] compared with the cost of a dozen pewter plates for 3*s* in 1312.[10]

With the general development of craft guilds in the 14th century the pewter industry revived and pewter, although expensive, was used in the homes of both nobility and middle classes in increasing amounts.

Forms of vessels are dictated by usage. Medieval food was of two main types — the spoonmeats or pottages, served in individual bowls or deep dishes and eaten with a spoon, and the finger foods sometimes called 'lechemeats' (sliced) such as beef or venison steaks broiled on a griddle, fritters and

fried confections of eggs or perhaps gingerbread. Forks were not in general use in England before the 17th century, so food was picked up with the fingers from large serving platters and placed upon square bread trenchers (Fr. *tranchoirs* from *tranche*, a slice) sliced from a four-day-old loaf. The aristocracy sometimes had silver-gilt or silver trenchers placed beneath their trencher bread, and in imitation humbler people eventually adopted wooden trenchers. These were in existence contemporaneously with trenchers of bread until at least the 16th century. Pewter trenchers would have been round, square, or rectangular, rimless or with wide low rounded rims (and then called plate trenchers). Trenchers survived into the 19th century, long after the introduction of pewter plates.

Pewter was easily scored by knives and the occupation of trencher scraper and pewter scourer was introduced in large households. Abrasive dust or sand was used to polish out any cut or scratch, or a specially designed tool could be used.[11] Fine polishing was done with horse-tail rush or pewterwort.[12]

The earliest extant item of domestic pewter is a spice plate or saucer of *c*1290 excavated from a stone-lined cesspit at Cuckoo Lane, Southampton and now at Southampton City Museum.[13] It has a strengthening beaded edge above the rim, which is punched with a Gothic letter 'P', the significance of which is as yet unknown, but which is possibly either a maker, owner or quality mark. The saucer would have been used to serve dried fruits such as raisins, currants and figs, or the pungent liquid condiments and sauces required to disguise the taste of food of varying freshness. One of the earliest surviving spoons[14] dating to approximately the same period (late 13th-early 14th century) has a stem reinforced with an iron wire; two knops are threaded onto the stem and soldered. (See also the ball knop spoon, *Catalogue* no.17c.) Most pewter spoons were cast integrally with their decorative knop.

After the Black Death in 1348, the greatly re-

Fig. 34. *(left)* Tavern Scene, woodcut dated 1641. From the Thomason Tracts (BL). Complaints of recent restraints on drinking, potting and piping on the Sabbath. *(Guildhall Library, City of London)*

Fig. 35. *(right)* The House of Rest, Wynkyn de Worde, woodcut from Pierre Gringore, *Castell of Laboure*, 1505. No. 1217 in *English Woodcuts 1480–1530* by Edward Hodnett, (OUP 1973)

duced population (from some 4 to 2½ million) enjoyed an enhanced prosperity. As the 14th century progressed and the pewter industry flourished, documentary sources reveal a range of domestic pewter platters, basins, pitchers, candlesticks, flagons and salts (salt cellars)[15] complimenting other vessels of wood, horn, pottery and leather. Occasionally the existence of more unusual items are revealed. In 1368 Thomas Kyneball, rector of St Martin Pomeroy, London, included a pewter pot 'for Vineger' (perhaps resembling a cruet in his church?) among the contents of his kitchen.[16] Neither was pewter restricted to London's merchant or middling class at this date: in 1377 John Brice, a farmer of Clee Stanton, Devon, left among his goods 'two chargers, seven dishes with five pewter saucers'.[17]

Household inventories, accounts and household management for the 15th century reveal that flatware, *ie* chargers (of up to 7*lbs* in weight), platters (2 to 2½*lbs*), dishes (13*oz* to 1½*lbs*), saucers 5 ⅓*oz* to 12*oz*)[18] and the like, were the most common pewter forms. Strict weights were specified for all flatware items and this appears the distinguishing feature. These items are also known as sadware, possibly from 'sad' meaning dense, heavy; medieval dishes are characteristically thick and weighty. Recent finds of saucers, dishes and a rare bowl or deep saucer[19] (probably for sauces or broth) from the Thames foreshore have added considerably to our knowledge of medieval flatware.

The second most important category of pewter utensil was for storage and drinking. These rarely survive, although various kinds of 'pots' (a generic term) are referred to in the richer inventories of the 14th and 15th centuries.[20] Measures ranged in size from the gallon (2 pottels) to the half pint and were made of two types — round and 'square',[21] *ie* of hexagonal or octagonal section made up of the appropriate number of shaped segments of flat sheet soldered together (so avoiding the use of expensive multi-part moulds). A mid-14th century quart octagonal flagon from the River Medway at Tonbridge, Kent, (*Catalogue* no.12) and another of

pottle capacity (½ gallon) from Abbots Leigh, Bristol (and now in the collections of Bristol City Museum), are of this form and were probably used for taking wine from cask to table. Both are of fine quality metal. Evidence of their use in London comes from an octagonal lid (now lacking the flagon body) with twin acorn thumbpiece and octagonal knop — found at Billingsgate and now privately owned.

The Mayor's precept of 1423[22] that all ale sold retail should be served in pewter pots of stamped capacity (to eliminate fraud) must have been a major boost to the craft. The earliest recognisable form of English pewter measure is that known as the baluster measure. A lidded hammerhead baluster measure of quart capacity recovered from the Thames foreshore and attributed to the second half of the 15th century is the earliest thus identified, although it is more likely to have contained wine than ale. The measure has a body conventionally made from halves joined round the middle and was doubtless of a type produced in quantity in a multi-part metal mould. It conformed to the type of 'round' measure, as specified in the 1348 Company regulations.[23] A similar squat measure was found on the *Mary Rose*, Henry VIII's warship, which sank in 1545 (*Catalogue* no.100). Their shapes are reminiscent of medieval copper alloy and pottery jugs. This bellied shape is perhaps the first in a sequence of shapes to be followed by slender 16th century forms, some of which can be dated independently by identical touchmarks as appear on mid-16th century spoons. This slimline 16th century shape was in turn followed by the squat form again from the mid-17th century (*Catalogue* nos.101–105).

According to the Company's 1348 regulations, other 'rounded vessels' made included candlesticks. Pewter candlesticks are rare by comparison with those of copper alloy or iron. A recent find from the Thames foreshore at Queenhithe was a socket candlestick, the stem and base cast in one piece. It appears to be the earliest known example of a functional medieval candlestick (*Catalogue* no.18).

The growth of luxury and increase in comfort which the 'middling' sort began first to enjoy during the 15th century is indicated by yet more plentiful supplies of pewter in the household, with individual plates, including those underneath trencher bread, salts, porringers and in particular with the inclusion in inventories of garnishes or sets of pewter for the first time as such. Dressers for the ostentatious display of plate were becoming a required feature, and the garnish of brightly burnished pewter was an obvious candidate when silver was too expensive. No garnish of medieval pewter survives although a hoard of some twenty plates, ranging in size from 10–14*in* and about 1*lb* in weight, was found on the site of Guy's Hospital, London. The rims are stamped with a crowned feather, believed to represent the device of Prince Arthur, eldest son of Henry VII (*Catalogue* no.27).

London platters were famous for their superior make, and were coveted even by the housewives of the North.[24] In the 16th century the Revd William Harrison wrote of the esteem in which pewter was held: 'Such furniture of household of this mettall [*ie* pewter] as we commonly call by the name of vessell is sold usually by the garnish, which doth contain twelve platters, twelve dishes, twelve saucers and those are either of silver fashion, or els with broad or narrow rims, and brought by the pound, which is now valued at six or seven pence, or peradventure at eight pence...In some places beyond the sea a garnish of good flat English pewter of an ordinary making...is esteemed almost so precious as the like number of vessels that are made of fine silver and in manner no less desired among the great estates, whose workmen are nothing so skilfull in that trade as ours, neither their metal so good, nor plenty so great, as we have here in England'.[25]

It was not always the case that nobles were served in silver-gilt. The high board groaned beneath a prodigious weight of gold and silver in the banqueting halls of Greenwich and York Place, but in the privacy of the Star Chamber, even the luxurious Wolsey and the noble Somerset were content to hire a garnish of pewter for the repast.[26] Many pewterers kept large stocks for hire. In 1505 the Lord Mayor's feast required over nine thousand pieces of pewter, of which three thousand were platters.[27]

On this occasion the drinking vessels were of pottery, ash and 'stone', indicating an area of competition to pewter at the beginning of the 16th century. Many new pottery types were being introduced by English potters, such as cups, beakers and other drinking vessels in attractive glazes, whilst 'stone' or stoneware jugs associated with the Rhenish wine trade were a popular import. This flourishing trade may partly explain the lack of pewter drinking vessels at this period, although cost was a critical factor, as always. An unskilled labourer, receiving 4*d* a day in wages, could purchase one dozen earthenware pots for the price of one pewter pot at 6*d*.[28]

Pewter lids were imported for mounting on pottery jugs in London and were subsequently made here. A stoneware jug of *c*1500 from Siegburg excavated in Exeter[29] is rare in having its associated lid, which more usually became detached and lost (unlike contemporary silver examples). In 1558 the Frenchman Etienne Perlin wrote: 'The English drink beer, not out of glasses, but from earthenware pots, the covers and handles being made of silver for the rich, the middle classes mount theirs in tin; the poorer sort use beer pots made of wood'.[30] The tradition of drinking from earthen and stoneware vessels continued through the 17th century, although by then the pewter tankard had been introduced for the same purpose.

It has been pointed out that expansion of production was a phenomenon of the pottery industry

Fig. 36. Domestic Interior, F. van Aken, early 18th century. (*Witt Library, Courtauld Institute of Art*)

around 1500.[31] This was equally the case of other industries, including pewter, and the range of objects expanded to meet the demand. From the middle of the 16th century the evidence of inventories suggest that pewter was being used in at least half the households in England. The average number of pieces per household ranged from almost fifteen in mid-16th century Nottinghamshire to some six in mid-17th century Essex, to quote only two examples.[32] What types of pewter would such households have owned? Early 16th century inventories list chargers, platters, dishes, garnishes, saucers, basins, porringers, 'pots' of various sizes and salts,[33] all being familiar from the 15th century. Surviving examples are few, although becoming more widely known from excavation and chance finds: plates (such as those from Guy's Hospital), saucers, porringers with three and four-lobed or fleur-de-lys twin handles, measures and large numbers of spoons.

The discovery of pewter aboard the *Mary Rose* has helped us date other pieces more precisely, notably dishes and porringers. The ship contained some new and exciting forms including screw-topped flasks, a sophisticated syringe and a flagon on a standing foot.[34] This type of wine flagon was familiar on the Continent from the 14th century and such vessels are known to have been made by at least one English pewterer.[35] They appear occasionally in richer English inventories, for example that of Edward Barton, apprentice haberdasher in 1543, who was buried at St Thomas, College Hill, London, which included 'a pot of pewter with a standing foot'.[36] Medieval toys of similar form have also been found in London (*Catalogue* no.19). A similar flagon, attributed to the mid-16th century, is known from the Hitchin area,[37] and further examples are that from Woodeaton Church, Oxon, (*Catalogue* no.42) and those in private ownership (*Catalogue* no.41). Pottle (or potel) measures of this form appear in the Exchequer Standard of 1496. This is the earliest known dated English representation of such vessels (*fig. 38* and *Catalogue* no.25).

In keeping with their idea of using secular forms to demystify ritual in the church, Protestant reformers introduced flagons to bring unconsecrated wine to the communion table. They were in use from at least 1547 when the laity was readmitted to Holy Communion, but greatly increased in numbers after 1603 when their use was further regularised. The Church then ordered that sacramental wine be 'brought to the communion table in a clean and sweet standing pot or stoup of pewter'.[38] Of all communion vessels, flagons survive in the greatest quantity, probably because of their size and value as well as the reverence with which they were treated. The types of 17th century flagon are further discussed below. Plates and alms dishes for ecclesiastical use were also made of pewter, several of which survive.

Between 1580 and 1620 a housing revolution swept through the English countryside, although with varied results in different regions. Rents and food prices were high, so yeomen farmers and land owners thrived. The parlour served increasingly as a display case for the products of material success. Here on the court cupboard was displayed the family's 'plate' — its silver, pewter and glassware. To quote William Harrison's celebrated passage

Fig. 37. From the Memorial Picture to Sir Henry Unton, *c*1596 (detail), English School. (*The National Portrait Gallery, London*)

and his account (1577) of the 'three things marvellously altered in England' within the memory of the eldest of his parishioners at Radwinter, Essex, the first two things commented on were the great increase in numbers of 'chymneys' and the general improvement of furnishings. He goes on: 'The third thing they tell of is the exchange of vessel, as of treen [wooden] platters into pewter, and wooden spoons into silver or tin. For so common were all sorts of treen stuff in old time that a man should hardly find four pieces of pewter (of which one was peradventure a salt) in a good farmer's house...'.[39] Pewter was now becoming plentiful in ordinary homes; allusions are found in Shakespeare to the use of pewterware in the household and to drinking vessels of that material in public houses and inns.[40] In 1599 David Hewett, pewterer and coiner of Rye had a range of over sixty vessels in his house. These included twenty-one assorted drinking vessels, an assortment of twenty-eight plates, platters, dishes, saucers, bowls and basins and a pewter beaker, a bottle, two kettles, five salts, and eight chamberpots.[41] Featured among the possessions of Richard Wowan of Rye in 1590 were a goblet, spoons, trenchers and a 'nut trimmed with pewter', and two pewter candlesticks and two pewter flower pots were among the goods of Robert Horsley, distrained for house rent in 1566.[42]

Inventories prepared after the death of testators

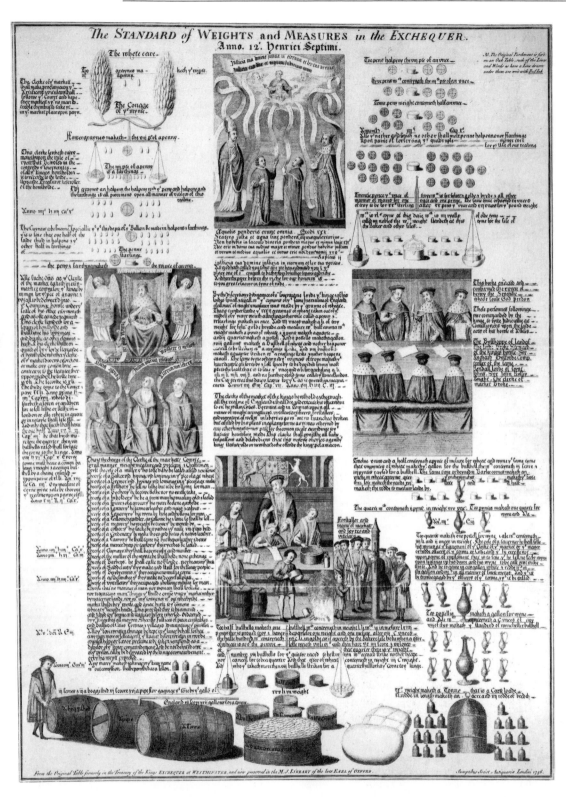

in the 16th and 17th centuries give us some idea of pewter holdings. Naturally ownership varied with wealth, occupation and region and there are, perhaps, no wholly representative inventories. However pewter was to be found amongst the wealthy and the poor, as the list of two Banbury men confirm.[43] The inventories were prepared within two days of each other in February 1557/8. Deans Anstie died worth only 14s 8d but amongst his few possessions were 'five pieces of pewter and a canstick' worth 1s 6d. His most valuable posses-

sions were three pairs of sheets at 3s the lot. On the other hand John Hasker left an estate of slightly over £93 and amongst this were four dozen items of pewter worth £1 10s and there may have been other pieces of pewter amongst the candlesticks and chamber pots recorded. Many further examples from other counties and periods confirm the size of pewter holdings after 1550 and the fact that domestic pewter was to be found in the homes of most people other than the very poor.

Only the flames from the fireplace, oil and rush

lamps and candles provided light after sunset. Candles made from tallow (mutton or beef fat) smelled, smoked and dripped when lighted, their low melting temperature caused them to droop easily, hence the use of a drip tray half way up the candlestick stem (*Catalogue* nos.51, 53, 54). Twisted wicks of linen which were not consumed by the flame also smoked, causing the tallow to spatter and necessitating the use of a snuffer. Richard Wowan's candlesticks were probably either bell-based or, as new evidence suggests, 'bawle'-knopped (*Catalogue* no.52). Although a great variety of other styles were made about 1600 few have survived today. The forms of 17th century pewter candlesticks, although showing a great deal of variety in detail, did not greatly change until the end of the century. They followed closely the patterns of contemporary types of silver. As the quality of wax improved so the drip tray was abandoned *c*1700. After this date pewter candlesticks virtually vanish until the late 18th century, driven out by the popularity of brass.

The moulds for casting the bases of drip tray type candlesticks were sometimes used for casting the attractive wide octagonal collar salts of about 1660. These gave way to capstan salts which, plain, continued to about 1675, then gadrooned, to around 1700. As the custom of intimate dining in small rooms gradually replaced dining in halls with a high table, great salts were displaced or augmented by these smaller trencher salts placed near the individual's trencher or plate. Most surviving salts are of the post-Restoration period. Designs of salts rapidly changed; they became old-fashioned and were consequently melted down for re-fashioning. (Since old pewter was valued at three-quarters of the price of new in the 17th century such costs were no obstacle.)[44]

English pewter is very restrained in its decoration. Two punched decorated plates survive from the 1580s in the collections of the Pewterers' Company and British Museum. This style of decoration continued until the late 17th century (*Catalogue* no.116) and is similar to punched decoration on leather. For two decades, from *c*1590–1610, a small amount of ornate cast decoration was produced following European traditions. Only a few pieces now survive and it is entirely appropriate that one of these, a fashionable standing cup, bears the arms of the Pewterers' Company (*Catalogue* no.106). This inspiration fitted well with the flamboyant taste of the time, as did the fashion for wriggleworked designs on pewter after the Restoration (*Catalogue* nos.122–132).

Plates were in common use by the early 17th century although few surviving examples can be attributed accurately to the first few decades of the century. Plates were lighter and smaller than dishes. They were used for individual consumption rather than as serving platters. Pewter plates with broad rims were in use in the 16th century and were abundant from 1640–90. Plain rims, or triple and multiple reedings incised or cast on narrow-rimmed plates, were a fashion from 1675–1700, when the simpler single-reeded rim appeared. Dishes and chargers ranged in diameter from 14 to 22*in.* Their function, as referred to by Randle Holme in 1688, was two-fold: 'both for necessary use (as putting of meat into them) to serve up to tables; as also to adorn their country houses; and court cupboards; for they are not looked up to be of any great worth in personals, that have not many dishes and which pewter, brass, copper and tin ware; set round about a Hall, Parlour and Kitchen'.[45]

Fig. 39. (left) William Brooke, 10th Lord Cobham with his family, dated 1567. English School. (*Reproduced by permission of the Marquess of Bath, Longleat House, Warminster, Wilts*)

Fig. 40. (right) Frontispiece to *Philcothonista*, by Thomas Heywood. English woodcut, published 1635, showing flat lidded tankards. Traditionally it was thought that these did not appear until the 1660s but this suggests an earlier date.

The main growth area of pewter in the 17th century other than plates was drinking vessels. Ale and beer were still the national drinks. Beer was cheap in London costing 2*d* or 3*d* a quart in the taverns and 4*s* to 8*s* a barrel (*ie* 36 gallons). Ale (with no hops for flavouring) was a little cheaper but less stable. Cheapest of all was small beer: a light brew popular with children and as a summer drink. Mum, a heavy ale made from wheat and matured for two years, was the 17th century equivalent of porter or stout. There were more than a thousand ale houses within the square mile of the City of London in 1614 and in 1638 over four hundred taverns. Both had increased in numbers in 1660.[46] The only statistical evidence that we have of increased beer consumption concerns the period 1684–94, when the excise revenue from ale and beer shows a marked increase that can only be accounted for by a rise in consumption.[47] The general popularity of the drinks, together with a rapidly expanding population, may help explain the great increase in production of pewter tavern pots and measures from the 17th century although, as references in contemporary literature point out, treen drinking vessels were still in common use. In *Philocothonista* (1635) Thomas Heywood lists the types in use: 'Of drinking cups, divers and sundry sorts we have;...Mazers, broad-mouth'd dishes, noggins, whiskins, piggins, crinzes, ale bowls, wassell-bowls, court-dishes, tankards, kannes, from a pottle to a pint, from a pint to a gill...'. (*figs. 40 & 42*) Nevertheless, pewter appears to have been the material associated with serving beer and popular names for a tavern serving man were 'pewter carrier' or 'potman'.[48]

Whilst ale houses were the lowest in the social scale, Londoners of Samuel Pepys' class drank wine almost as freely as ale or beer both in taverns and at home. The provision of standard measures for use in ale houses and taverns had been a major part of the pewterers' business from the 14th century (see page 34). Indeed the first recorded case brought against a pewterer was on 29 June 1350 when 'twenty three measures, called potels [half-gallons] of false metal [*ie* the greater part of lead] made by John de Hiltone were seized [for destruction]'.[49] The form of baluster measure (slimline from the 16th century) had returned to a squat shape by 1650. Balusters remained little altered for another one hundred and fifty years, only the thumbpiece varying to any great extent (*Catalogue* nos.100–105).

Of all the types of 17th century pewter available, the lidded tankard is one of the most collected today. The word tankard originally signified a wooden vessel holding two gallons or more, and is probably derived from the Latin *cantharus* which led to the Old French *tanquard*; its capacity has been for at least two centuries in England either a quart, pint or half-pint. The tankard, with its cylindrical body and handle on one side, was already used in the 16th century, albeit of crystal or silver. Documentary references to pewter 'tanggad pots' date from 1482,[50] although one of the earliest extant examples is attributed to *c*1650–75 (*Catalogue* no.97) and follows a style of silver tankard of about 1630. During the remainder of the 17th century the main changes in tankard form were in the shapes of thumbpiece, the increase in height of the lid, and ornamentation and overall shape of the

drum, the last two being popular trends encouraged by examples in silver.[51] After the Restoration tankards were produced in large numbers and remained popular until the end of the 18th century. Although primarily a domestic form, the tankard also served for ceremonial and presentation purposes.

Fig. 41. Beer Street, 1750, engraving, William Hogarth. (*Museum of London*)

Fig. 42. The Pot Boy, English School, early 18th century. (*City of Bristol Museum and Art Gallery*)

Flagons were mainly used for holding unconsecrated wine at church services. The beefeater flagon, the first style after the Restoration, is so called because of the lid shape (*Catalogue* nos.48, 49). After about 1685 some flagons have a new appearance, with a flat lid derived from tankards and the body bearing two bands. Contemporary tavern mugs also have this hooped decoration.

Banded ornamentation appears to have been an attempt to simulate the hoops on wooden-staved drinking pots and measures. The thurdendale or hooped quart ale or beer measure (*Catalogue* no.39) is one of only two known examples. Such stave-built wooden drinking vessels were found, for example on the *Mary Rose*. Apparently thurdendales were made larger than standard capacity to allow for 'the working and ascending of the yeast and froth' of ale and beer.[52]

If thurdendales are rare today, tavern or pub mugs are one of the most frequent survivors and favourites amongst collectors. One of the earliest dated pewter tavern mugs is a quart with twin incised bands and a solid handle (*Catalogue* no.91). By the end of the century the twin incised bands on such tankards had become two or three bold bands or hoops (*Catalogue* nos.92, 93). An attractive variant to this design is the gadrooning or fluting seen on mugs of the early 18th century.

Amongst recent acquisitions by the Museum of London are two pewter bowls, one weighing 12⅔oz (359*gm*) and of *c*700*ml* capacity; in 1612/13 the Pewterers' Company ordered that 'small beere bowls' were to weigh 12 ⅓oz each. One bowl, dating from 1638, might be the first such to be recognised although they were in common usage in the early 17th century (*Catalogue* nos.84, 85). Drinking from shallow bowls or mazers had been a familiar custom since the medieval period.

Spurred on by the stimulus of replacing utensils lost in the Fire of London in 1666, keen competition from the pottery industry and changing fashions in a relaxed atmosphere after the Restoration of Charles II, large amounts of very attractive pewter were made in the fifty or so years to the end of Queen Anne's reign in 1714. This period was the high point of English pewter production in both design and workmanship, and pewterers encouraged business by many rapid changes in style. It has been estimated that in the 1680s the nation's stock of pewter was at its peak, with more households containing pewter than ever before due to the rising population and wider dissemination of wares.[53] However, as always, those who could afford it, spurned pewter for silver.

The manufacture of plates and dishes was greatly improved by the production of 'hard metal' or 'French pewter' — pewter containing antimony — introduced into England in the 1650s by James Taudin, a French Protestant refugee. Although considerably more expensive than the best quality pewter, it was extremely durable and rapidly achieved great popularity (*Catalogue* no.79). Flatware remained the type of pewter most in demand during the second half of the 17th century.

Caudle cups and porringers were much used in the late 17th and early 18th century. Pewter caudle cups may have one or two handles (also known as loving cups) and were used for drinking caudle, a warm drink made of wine or ale mixed with sugar, bread and spices; they followed the contemporary

silver styles. The same form of vessel was also used as a toasting cup from which wine was drunk at dinner, the cup being passed from hand to hand. The Pewterers' Company possesses a gadrooned commemorative loving cup of *c*1702 (*Catalogue* no.109); see also another by William Hux of London (*Catalogue* no.115).

Porringers (pottingers) were larger at the mouth than caudle cups. These multi-purpose utilitarian vessels, from which a wide variety of foods such as stews and puddings might be eaten, were first mentioned in the Company's records in 1348 (as Fr. *esquelles*).[54] The earliest existing examples can be securely dated no earlier than the mid-16th century, being amongst pewterware recovered from the wreck of the *Mary Rose* (1545). Porringers of this date have two ears of tri- or four-lobed form or fleur-de-lys. 17th century porringers commonly have a single ear. Relief casting was reintroduced with the influx of foreign pewterers who followed William of Orange to Britain. Sophisticated covered porringers of unusually wide diameter reflect the Continental tradition (*Catalogue* no.114), although the smooth surfaces of the handles are in a traditional English openwork pattern. Examples such as the commemorative porringers, and the fine wrigglework tankards and plates of the period show that pewter was not confined to a merely utilitarian role.

During the 17th and 18th centuries the use of pewter in Britain, apart from domestic plates, dishes, drinking pots and so on, was chiefly for feeding cups, feeding bottles (*Catalogue* no.71) and pap boats and for sick-room requisites: syringes, bed pans, chamber pots and urinals. Bleeding bowls with one handle, the interior showing graduation rings and containing up to 16 fluid ounces, are not uncommon. Pewter bowls were listed by chemists' sundriesmen as late as the beginning of

Fig. 43. Interior of a Tavern, after A. van Ostade, 17th century. (*Victoria and Albert Museum*)

Fig. 44. Behind the Bar, 1882, John Henry Henshall, watercolour. (*Museum of London*)

Fig. 45. A child with a feeding bottle, dated 1593, English School. (*Courtesy of Sotheby's, London*)

this century when one could still purchase pewter feeding bottles in 18th century shapes. Finds recovered from the barber-surgeon's chest on the *Mary Rose* include a pewter syringe with a bronze pipe. The needle has a small rounded nipple on the end for use in urethral injections for the treatment of bladder stones and for gonorrhoea. In addition, syringes could be used to treat wounds, ulcers and fistulae. The chest also included a series of graded pewter flasks, possibly to contain drugs or spirits (*Catalogue* no.35).

As well as these main categories of pewterware, small objects such as pewter toys (*Catalogue* no.26), miniature models of larger items, dog whistles, bird feeders, ink pots, jewellery, sugar crushers for rum drinkers, meat skewers, tobacco stoppers, candle snuffers and pewter snuff boxes, to mention only a few, were made by a specific branch of the trade known as tryfflers (from the alloy, or trifle used). As final uses of pewter at this period, may be mentioned emergency coinage as struck from the Commonwealth to the reign of William and Mary.

An investigation of the searches carried out by the Company for substandard ware in pewterers' shops reveals a number of rare items: scallop salts, salmon plates and salmon porringers (Gloucester search 1684), pasting plates (1662), brandy cups (1675), small teapots (1689), Betty pots (*ie* 1½ pint measures), knife shafts of pewter,[55] and aqua vitae and strong water bottles. No licence was required for selling spirits and by 1621 there were two hundred strong-water houses in London;[56] aqua vitae (made from fermented grain and occasionally wine lees) was the most common.

It is interesting to note the reference to pewter teapots in 1689, tea having first been introduced into England from China about 1658. The introduction of hot beverages (tea, coffee and chocolate) was detrimental to the pewter industry, the production of teapots and the accompanying tea cups, saucers and plates, being exploited by the pottery trade. It was not until the late 18th and 19th centuries that the Britannia Metal trade attempted to compete once more with pottery and

porcelain in the manufacture of tea and coffee sets. This new alloy (90% tin and 10% antimony) was at first used simply as an improved pewter but in the 19th century was generally plated.

Gradually pewter fell before the advances of new technology. Just as silver had to compete with electroplating, so the pewter trade, and then the Britannia Metal trade, lost ground to more fashionable materials, their most recent successors being stainless steel and plastic.

ROSEMARY WEINSTEIN
Keeper, Tudor & Stuart Dept.,
Museum of London.

Notes

THE PEWTERERS OF LONDON

1 Homer, pp. 138–9
2 Welch, vol. 1, pp2–5 and Riley, pp241–4, give alternative texts of the 1348 ordinances.
3 Homer, p145 gives estimated numbers of London pewterers at various dates
4 Homer, p138
5 Hatcher and Barker, pp34 and 42
6 Riley, pp123–4
7 Homer, pp139–40, for details of Nicholas and other early pewterers
8 Homer, p141
9 Riley, pp259–60
10 Sharpe (1894), Bk.G, pp171–3
11 Dawes, p170
12 Sharpe (1885), Roll 1, No. 207
13 Homer, p143
14 Welch, Vol. 1, p13
15 Homer, p145
16 Gairdner, letter 496
17 Sharpe (1894), Bk. 1, pp97–8
18 Hatcher, p170ff; Hatcher and Barker, p64
19 Homer, p142 citing Letter Book K, folio 49v
20 Homer, p142
21 Welch, vol. 1, pp20–5
22 Homer, pp146–7
23 Guildhall Ms. 22,156; see J. Pewter Soc. (14) for a transcript
24 Sellars
25 Cotterell, p7
26 Homer and Hall, for details of some provincial guilds
27 Guildhall Ms. 7086/1
28 Guildhall Ms. 22,199; see J. Pewter Soc. (19) for a transcript
29 19 Henry VII, Cap VI; see Welch pp94–7
30 Guildhall Ms. 22,204; see J. Pewter Soc. (11) for a transcript
31 J. Pewter Soc. (17)
32 Hatcher and Barker, pp270–4
33 Guildhall Ms. 22,198
34 Guildhall Ms. 7105
35 Guildhall Ms. 7090, 20 March 1711/12
36 Guildhall Ms. 22,223; see J. Pewter Soc. (10)
37 Universal Director, 1763
38 Welch, vol. 2, pp61–4, 147–9
39 Guildhall Ms. 22,202; see J. Pewter Soc. (18) for a transcript
40 Welch, vol. 2, p142
41 Hatcher and Barker, pp129–30
42 Guildhall Ms. 22,209; see J. Pewter Soc. (8) for a transcript

PEWTER MANUFACTURE

1 Hornsby, p11
2 Established in the 1348 Ordinances. Hatcher and Barker, p224
3 Hornsby, p12; J. Pewter Soc., (12)
4 Ordinances of Pewterers' Company 1348. Welch, Vol. 1, p6
5 Hatcher and Barker, p224
6 Hatcher and Barker, pp230–8 and 305–11
7 Hatcher and Barker, p221
8 The Pewter Society owns one of the few sets of holloware moulds to survive from the 18th century: a set of pint Jersey moulds
9 See collection of pewterer's tools in the Pewterers' Company collection
10 Hatcher and Barker, pp219–20

11 Hatcher and Barker, p220
12 Welch, vol. 1, pp34–5
13 Welch, vol. 1, p183
14 Welch, vol. 2, pp155 and 592
15 Cotterell includes over 6,000 examples of makers' marks
16 Cotterell, see especially marks of Bristol pewterers including Edgar, Page and Burgum pp171 & 277
17 Cotterell, for example see mark no. 1475 used by Durand father and son
18 Hornsby, pp29–31, 37–8
19 Hornsby, pp41–6
20 Hatcher and Barker, table 12
21 Hatcher and Barker, tables 12 and 13
22 Hornsby Ms. (a)
23 Welch, vol. 1, pp175 and 252
24 For example no items of flatware have survived made by the noted flagon maker EG (c1600–30)
25 Hatcher and Barker, tables 12–14
26 Hatcher and Barker, p247
27 Homer and Hall, pp5–8
28 Hatcher and Barker, p248; Homer and Hall, p7
29 Welch, vol. 1, p15 (1448: Welch wrongly attributes this to 1451)
30 Welch, vol. 1, p105
31 Welch, vol. 1, p165
32 Hatcher and Barker, p249
33 Douch, for details of individual Cornish pewterer's inventories
34 Homer and Hall, for details of individual provincial pewterer's inventories
35 ibid.
36 ibid.
37 ibid.
38 ibid.
39 Hornsby Ms. (b)

BUYING AND SELLING PEWTER

1 Hatcher and Barker, table 12
2 Hornsby Ms. (a)
3 Hatcher and Barker, p128; Guildhall Ms. 7105; J. Pewter Soc. (9)
4 ibid.
5 Guildhall Ms. 7105
6 Hatcher and Barker, table 14
7 Hatcher and Barker, pp70–5 and 124
8 Cotterell
9 For example recent research has identified many more provincial makers. See J. Pewter Soc. (3), (7), (13) and (15)
10 Hatcher and Barker, p141
11 Tawney
12 Hollis (ed)
13 Hatcher and Barker, p276
14 Hornsby Ms. (b)
15 J. Pewter Soc. (1)
16 Beveridge, pp85–90
17 For example, Welch, vol. 1, pp94–7 and 254–5
18 J. Pewter Soc. (5)
19 P.R.B. E 190 series
20 P.R.B. E 190.187.665.13
21 P.R.B. E 190.187.663.15
22 Byrne (ed); pp67–8
23 Chirk Accounts, 1666–1753, Manchester, 1931

24 Sotheby's sale catalogue, 1 June 1956
25 Bunyard
26 Guildhall Ms. 7105
27 *ibid.*
28 Hatcher and Barker, fig. 5.1
29 Hatcher and Barker, fig. 5.2
30 Hatcher and Barker, fig. 5.3
31 Furnivall (ed), p34
32 Addison, for a general discussion of the role of fairs
33 Guildhall Ms. 7105; J. Pewter Soc. (9)
34 Guildhall Ms. 7105
35 *ibid.*
36 *ibid.*
37 Defoe, pp102–7
38 Hatcher and Barker, p185
39 Welch, vol 2, pp68–9 and 119
40 Welch, vol. 1, pp226 and 246
41 Welch, vol. 1, pp44 and 131–2
42 Welch, vol. 2, p8

PEWTER: ITS DEVELOPMENT AND USE

1 Whitelock, pts 1–2, p292; discussed by Homer, J. Pewter Soc. (16)
2 Homer, p138
3 Simpson, p300
4 Hatcher and Barker, p29
5 Sneyd, p29
6 Hatcher and Barker, p29
7 Spencer, p10
8 Stevenson
9 Lyons
10 Rogers, vol. 2, p569
11 Welch, vol. 2, p155
12 Pewter–wort: the plant *Equisetum hyemale*, 1597 Gerarde *Herbal*, p958 'Italian rushie Horse taile. Women scowre their pewter and wooden things of the kitchen therewith and thereupon some of our huswives do call it Pewterwort.'
13 Platt, vol. 2, pp250–2; also Alexander and Binski, p. 280 no. 208
14 Now in collection of Worshipful Company of Pewterers
15 Hatcher and Barker, pp54–5
16 Thomas, p92
17 Public Record Office SC.2.160/25; and Hatcher and Barker, p58
18 Hatcher and Barker, p55; Homer, p142 inventory of Thomas Filkes, pewterer in 1427
19 See also Allan, p.345
20 Hatcher and Barker, p55
21 Welch, vol. 1, p3 (Company regulations 1348)
22 Herbert, vol. 1, p58
23 Welch, vol. 1, p3 (Company regulations 1348)
24 Raine, vol. 3, p219
25 Harrison, p367
26 British Library Ms Lansdown, no. 1, fol. 118
27 Furnivall, pp363–4
28 Rogers, vol. 3, pp544–82; Hatcher and Barker, p62
29 Allan, p160, no. 1729
30 E.B. Pack, 'Tigerware Jugs', *Antiques 39* (April 1941), pp176–7
31 G.J. Dawson, 'Excavations at Guy's Hospital', *Research Volume of the Surrey Archaeol. Soc.* No. 7, 1979, especially section: 'The ceramic revolution'. Microfiche 241–5
32 Hatcher and Barker, p96
33 Hatcher and Barker, pp56–7
34 On view at the Mary Rose Trust, Portsmouth
35 Edward Glover (active 1611–20), J. Pewter Soc. (6). His mark shows such a vessel.
36 Darlington, pp100–1
37 On display at Hitchin Museum, Herts and referred to in J. Pewter Soc. (2)
38 Massé, p93
39 Harrison, pp201–2
40 Shakespeare: 1596 *Taming of the Shrew* Act ii. sc. 1, 357 'Pewter and brass and all things that belong to house or house keeping'. 1596: *Henry IV*, ii, Act iv. sc. 5.1. 'Five years Berlady a long Lease fro the clinking of pewter'.
41 Mayhew, p183
42 Mayhew, p183
43 Havinden, nos. 201 and 202
44 Hatcher and Barker, p90
45 Holme, p4
46 Latham and Matthews, vol. 10, pp104–7
47 Latham and Matthews, p104
48 Marryat, vol. 2
49 Riley, pp259–60
50 Welch, vol. 1, p57
51 See for example Peal, Chapter 8
52 'The Assize and Order of Inhalers and Victuallers', c1600, in J. Powell (Clerk of the Market at the time of Queen Elizabeth and James I) *Assize of Bread 1684* unpaginated
53 Hatcher and Barker, p141
54 Riley, pp241–4
55 J. Pewter Soc. (4)
56 Latham and Matthews p106 (Commons Debates 1621)

Bibliography

* Indicates books quoted in the *Catalogue* (pages 48–111). Books which are quoted only once in the *Catalogue* and articles in journals and magazines, are given there in full and are not listed in this bibliography, which relates primarily to the essays on pp10–41.

ADDISON W. Addison, *English Fairs and Markets*, 1953

ALEXANDER AND BINSKI *J. Alexander and P. Binski (eds), *Age of Chivalry, Art in Plantagenet England 1200–1400*, Royal Academy, London, 1987, exhibition catalogue

ALLAN J. Allan, *Medieval and Post–Medieval Finds from Exeter 1971–80*, 1984

BEVERIDGE W. Beveridge, *Prices in England from the 12th to 19th Centuries*, 1939

BUNYARD B. Bunyard, *Brokerage Book of Southampton, 1439–40*, 1941

BYRNE M. St. C. Byrne (ed), *Lisle Letters*, 1983

COTTERELL *H.H. Cotterell, *Old Pewter its Makers and Marks*, 1929

*H.H. Cotterell, *Pewter Down the Ages*, 1932

*Cotterell, Riff and Vetter, *National Types of Old Pewter*, revised 1972

DARLINGTON I. Darlington (ed), *London Consistory Court Wills 1492–1547*, London Record Society, 1967

DAWES M.C.B. Dawes (ed), *Register of the Black Prince, 1351–65*, 1930

DEFOE Daniel Defoe, *A Tour through the Whole Island of Great Britain*, repr. Penguin, 1971

DOUCH H.L. Douch, *Cornish Pewterers*, Journal, Royal Institute of Cornwall, 1969, New Series, vol. VI, part 1

FURNIVALL F.J. Furnivall (ed), *Harrison's Elizabethan England*, Scott Library

F.J. Furnivall (ed), *Early English Meals and Manners*, Early English Text Society, 1868

GAIRDNER J. Gairdner (ed), *The Paston Letters*, 1904, 6 vols.

GUILDHALL MS. 7105 *Record Books of Company Searchers, 1635–41 and 1669–83*

GUILDHALL MS. Manuscripts at Guildhall Library, London

HARRISON William Harrison, *The Description of England*, ed. G. Edelen, 1968

HATCHER J. Hatcher, *English Tin Production and Trade before 1550*, 1973

HATCHER AND BARKER *J. Hatcher and T.C. Barker, *A History of British Pewter*, 1974

HAVINDEN M.A. Havinden (ed), *Household and Farm Inventories in Oxfordshire, 1550–90*, 1965

HERBERT W. Herbert, *The Twelve Great Livery Companies*, 1834–6, 2 vols.

HOLLIS Hollis (ed), *Bristol Pewterers, Calendar of Bristol Apprentices Records 1532–65*, Bristol Record Society XIV, 1949

HOLME Randle Holme, *An Academie or Store House of Armory and Blazon*, 1688

HOMER R.F. Homer, 'The Medieval Pewterers of London'. *Trans.* London and Middlesex Archaeol. Soc. vol. 36, pp137–62 (1985), 1988

*R.F. Homer, *Five Centuries of Base Metal Spoons*, 1975

HOMER AND HALL R.F. Homer and D. Hall, *Provincial Pewterers*, 1985

HORNSBY MS. P.R.G. Hornsby manuscripts: (a) *Bristol Pewterers*, 1978; (b) *Survey of Pewter in 16th and 17th century inventories*, 1978

*P.R.G. Hornsby, *Pewter, Copper and Brass*, 1981

HORNSBY *P.R.G. Hornsby, *Pewter of the Western World*, 1983

J. PEWTER SOC. *Journal of the Pewter Society*. Articles quoted in the essays on pp10–41 have been numbered for easy reference in this bibliography.

(1) R.F. Homer, 'Clothworkers' Pewter', vol. 1, Spring 1977, pp24–30

(2) C.A. Peal, 'Pewter from the Mary Rose', vol. 2, Autumn 1979, pp22–3

(3) 'Wigan Pewterers', vol. 2, Spring 1980, pp15–20

(4) Stanley Shemmell, 'Re–examination of the records of the Pewterers' Company', vol. 2, Spring 1980, pp. 27–33

(5) P.R.G. Hornsby, 'The Marketing of Pewter in the 17th century', vol. 3, Spring 1981, p10

(6) 'Pear–shaped flagons', vol. 3, Spring 1982, pp73–5

(7) A.S. Law, 'Birmingham Pewterers of the 17th century', vol. 3, Autumn 1982, pp128–32

(8) R.F. Homer, 'Tinplate Workers', vol. 4, Spring 1983, pp17–18

(9) R.F. Homer, 'Pewter Company Search 1692', vol. 4, Autumn 1983, pp61–4

(10) R.F. Homer, 'The Story of James Taudin', vol. 4, Autumn 1984, pp118–22

(11) R.F. Homer, 'The Unemployed Journeymen's Petition', vol. 5, Spring 1985, pp13–14

(12) R. Brownsword and E. Pitt, 'Pewter Analysis', vol. 5, Autumn 1985, pp44–8

(13) D.F. Hall and R.F. Homer, 'Exeter Pewterers', vol. 5, Spring 1986, pp76–7

(14) R.F. Homer, 'The Pewterers' Ordinances of 1455', vol. 5, Spring 1986, pp101–6

(15) 'Norwich Pewterers and Braziers', vol. 6, Spring 1987, pp5–7

(16) R.F. Homer, 'The Earliest Mention of English Pewter', vol. 6, Spring 1987, pp12–13

(17) R.F. Homer, 'More About the Unemployed Journeymen of London', vol. 6, Spring 1987, pp22–3

(18) R.F. Homer, 'The Pewterers' Company Rules of 1639', vol. 6, Autumn 1987, pp72–3

(19) R.F. Homer, 'The Pewterers' Company vs John Whitehead, 1478', vol. 6, Spring 1988, pp92–5

LATHAM AND MATTHEWS R.C. Latham and W. Matthews (ed), *The Diary of Samuel Pepys*, (vol. 10, Companion, 1983)

LYONS S. Lyons, 'Extracts from the Rotulus Familiae 18, Edward I', *Archaeologia* XV (1806)

MARRYAT F. Marryat, *Peter Simple*, 1834

MASSÉ H.J.L.J. Massé, *Pewter Plate*, 1910

*H.J.L.J. Massé, *Chats on Old Pewter*, rev. 1949

MAYHEW G. Mayhew, *Tudor Rye*, 1987

MICHAELIS *R.F. Michaelis, *Antique Pewter of the British Isles*, 1955

*R.F. Michaelis, *British Pewter*, 1969

*R.F. Michaelis, *Old Domestic Base Metal Candlesticks from the 13th to 19th Century*, 1978

*Museum of London, *Pewter*, 1983, a handbook

P.R.B. *The Port Record Books*, Public Records Office

PEAL *C.A. Peal, *Pewter of Great Britain*, 1983

*C.A. Peal, *British Pewter and Britannia Metal for Pleasure and Investment*, 1971

PLATT R. Coleman–Smith Platt, *Excavations in Medieval Southampton 1953–69*, 1975

RAINE J. Raine (ed), *Wills and Inventories Illustrative of the History, Manners, Language, Statistics, etc. of the Northern Counties of England from the Eleventh Century Onwards*, Surtees Society, 1835–1929

RILEY H.T. Riley (ed), *Memorials of London and London Life in the XIII, XIV and XVth Centuries*, 1868

ROGERS J.E.T. Rogers, *A History of Agriculture and Prices in England, 1866–1902*, 7 vols. Finchale Priory Accounts

SELLARS M. Sellars (ed), *York Memorandum Book*, Surtees Society, 1911

SHARPE (1885) R.R. Sharpe (ed), *Calendar of Letters from the Mayor and Corporation of London*, 1885

SHARPE (1894) R.R. Sharpe (ed), *Calendar of Letter Books pre-*served among the Archives of the City of London, 1894–1912, 12 vols

SIMPSON W.S. Simpson (ed), 'Visitations of certain Churches in the patronage of St. Paul's Cathedral Church between the years 1138 and 1250', *Archaeologia* IV, pt. 2, 1897

SNEYD C.A. Sneyd (ed), *Italian Relation of England: a relation or rather a true account of the Island of England*, Camden Society, XXXVII, 1847

SPENCER 'A Thirteenth Century Pilgrim's Ampulla from Worcester', *Worcs. Archaeol. Soc. Trans.*, 1984

STEVENSON Joseph Stevenson (ed), *Documents Illustrative of the History of Scotland, 1286–1306*, 1870

TAWNEY A.J. and R.H. Tawney, 'An Occupational Census of the 17th Century', *Economic History Review*, 1934–5

THOMAS A.H. Thomas (ed), *Calendar of Plea and Memoranda Rolls...at the Guildhall AD1364–1381*, 1929

ULLYETT *K.A. Ullyett, *Pewter Collecting for Amateurs*, 1967

WELCH C. Welch, *History of the Worshipful Company of Pewterers*, 1902, 2 vols.

WHITELOCK D. Whitelock (*et al*) (ed), *Councils and Synods, with other documents relating to the English Church AD871–1204*, 1981.

*The Worshipful Company of Pewterers, *Catalogue of Pewterware*, 1968, and *Supplementary*, 1979

Dating Pewter

It is not easy to date pewter precisely. There is relatively little archaeological evidence and that which does exist relates to the period prior to 1500, when pewter was uncommon. We are therefore left with two important ways of dating an object, marks and style, coupled with other factors such as alloy, method of manufacture and identification of ownership.

MARKS

Considerable help can be obtained where items are marked with a maker's name or device. The mark of a pewterer is known as his touch, but the term 'maker's mark' is commonly used. Unfortunately the touchplates on which London pewterers struck their marks were destroyed in the Great Fire and we only have the plates from 1666 to guide us. There are no provincial touchplates or books recording marks. Thus even where marks do exist it is not always possible to identify the maker.

The type of marks used by pewterers have varied over time, so that the nature and style of the touch can give some indication as to age. Early maker's marks are simple and often struck incuse, that is into the surface of the pewter. Later marks are struck so that parts of the design can be felt if the finger is rubbed over its surface.

The first recorded marks are those of the pewterer's hammer — probably a sign of quality or an indication that the item was made by a guild member. It is thought that the hammer was also used by provincial makers as well as those from London. Later a crown was added to the hammer mark and it is possible that this occurred after the granting of the Royal Charter in 1473/4 although there is not direct evidence to confirm this hypothesis. European pewterers also used the hammer mark in the 14th and 15th centuries. Another group of early marks include a crowned rose. This is sometimes confused with the mark found on Dutch pewter to indicate the use of English tin, but the crowned rose mark with maker's initials was employed in this country for some time before its adoption in Holland. It is likely that in the late 15th century other simple maker's marks were used. There is a hoard of pewter with the Prince of Wales feathers struck on the rim (*Catalogue* no.27) and some of these have a simple bell mark. Other plain devices with or without initials also appear to date from this period. These basically simple and limited marks gradually gave way to marks incorporating the initials of the maker. Many marks can be found stamped in beaded circles, first used before 1600.

The 17th century saw the development of more complex marks, often incorporating the full name of the maker. Marks tended to become larger as the century progressed.

OWNERSHIP AND CAPACITY MARKS

In addition to maker's marks some help in dating can be obtained from owners' initials. The style of lettering in which they are punched or engraved can assist with dating. The way inscriptions and coats-of-arms are engraved can also be useful as the style employed varied in different periods. There are also official capacity marks added to the holloware used as ale or wine measures. These stamps can assist in dating but can confuse, however, as the 'HR' mark for Henry VII continued in service into the 17th century and the 'WR' mark for William III standards continued in use for many years.

Fig. 46. Mark of a pewterer's hammer, *c*1400, from a spice plate found at Tong Castle, Shropshire

Fig. 47. Mark of a rose and crown, *c*1650, from a Maidenhead spoon

Fig. 48. 'Hallmarks' of Joseph Gidding, *c*1690, from a charger

Fig. 46

Fig. 47

Fig. 48

ALLOY

Where it is possible to sample the alloy used some aid can be obtained in dating an object. For example, bismuth was not intentionally used in English pewter prior to the late 17th century, antimony was only employed at trace levels before 1680, while copper, widely employed from the medieval period into the 17th century, was seldom incorporated in pewter thereafter.

STYLE

The style and design of objects are the most helpful features in dating pewter. Early students and writers on pewter tended to assume that design followed a chronological pattern, each new form replacing an earlier style and in turn being replaced by new designs, and they developed strict classifications based on this theory. There is evidence to show that, to a degree, this did occur.

In the 16th century, for example, the sloping sided deep plate was gradually replaced by a broad-rimmed plate of flatter form, and this in turn gave way in the 1680s to what is called a triple-reeded plate, the rim of which is incised or cast with reeding. In due course a range of narrow-rimmed plates became popular and then plates with a single-reeded or a plain rim evolved, which first appeared in the 1690s but are mainly 18th century forms. Initially it was thought that this progression was precise and exact, but we now appreciate, for example, that all the styles of 17th century plates overlapped to some degree. We know that broad-rimmed plates lasted for well over one hundred and fifty years and were manufactured for many years side by side with deeper sloping plates which were made over an even longer period. Whilst there are general changes in style which can be identified, they are not immutable: each style does not give way instantly to the new.

With most objects it is possible to identify changes of style, which can assist with dating. However it is essential that we remember that it is we who are establishing these classifications, not the original pewterers. It is all too easy to try and make stylistic changes fit into pre-conceived patterns. Such stylistic changes were caused, not by someone blowing a whistle, but by market factors such as costs, popular demand and the pressures of fashion. Individual makers will have gone on producing one style of object for a long time after other makers had abandoned it. Naturally where styles are known to have changed fast, as with pewter flagons, some additional precision can be achieved. Help can also be found to a limited degree in related trades, such as silver and brass. Contemporary drawings, paintings and book illustrations can also be of assistance, but regretfully this kind of material is more prevalent on the Continent than in this country.

The dating of pewter must rely on all these factors. Unless there is specific additional information such as inscribed dates or manuscript material, it is unwise to make any hypothesis on dating too precise.

P.R.G.H.

Fig. 49

Fig. 50

Fig. 51

Fig. 52

Fig. 53

Fig. 54

Fig. 55

Fig. 49. 'Hallmarks' of the maker 'WF' c1685, from a dish

Fig. 50. Mark for Superfine Hard Metal, London, c1740, from a flagon

Fig. 51. Touchmarks of William Cooke, Bristol, c1765

Fig. 52. Touchmarks of Thomas Alderson, c1820, from a George IV Coronation banquet plate

Fig. 53. Maker's touch 'LI', late 16th-early 17th century, from a spoon

Fig. 54. Capacity mark for William III, c1695

Fig. 55. Touchmark of Lawrence Child, c1695, from a porringer

The Catalogue

DOCUMENTS

The archives of the Worshipful Company of Pewterers exist from the middle of the 15th century onwards and are deposited in the Guildhall Library. The older ones survive through the heroic efforts of William Rawlins, one of the wardens, who rescued them from the Company's hall before it was engulfed in the fire of 1666 and stored them in two sea chests. These extensive and varied documents enable us to bring to life the activities of the London pewterers over many centuries.

1 INSTRUCTIONS FOR APPRENTICES

This 17th century printed leaflet bears a woodcut of the Company's arms and comprises a homily on good behaviour addressed to its apprentices. They are exhorted to serve God, to do diligent and faithful service to their masters, to avoid idleness, and be of fair, gentle, and lowly speech and behaviour to all men.
Guildhall ms. 22,165

2 APPRENTICESHIP INDENTURE

This indenture binds Richard Henson of Yelverstoft, Northamptonshire, as apprentice to Mary Priest, citizen and pewterer of London, for seven years from 14 October 1680 'to learn his art with her...her secrets keep [and] her lawful commandments everywhere gladly do'. It admonishes him not to commit fornication, marry, play at cards or dice, nor haunt taverns or playhouses. As will be apparent from this document, women were admitted to the freedom of the Company and practised as working pewterers.
Guildhall ms. 22,185

The sizes of nos. 1–6 are as follows: (1) 7¼ x 8″ (184 x 203mm), (2) 9 x 7″ (228 x 178mm), (3) 8½ x 13″ (215 x 330mm), (4) 23 x 33″ (584 x 838mm), (5) 16 x 12½″ (406 x 318mm), (6) 36 x 18″ (914 x 456mm).

Instructions for the Apprentices, in the City of *LONDON*.

YOU shall constantly and devoutly on your knees, every day, serve God Morning and Evening, and make Conscience in the due hearing of the Word Preached; and endeavour the right practice thereof in your Life and Conversation: You shall do diligent and faithful Service to your Master for the time of your Apprenticeship, and deal truly in what you shall be trusted: You shall often Read over the Covenants of your Indenture, and see and endeavour your self to perform the same to the uttermost of your power: You shall avoid all evil Company, and all Occasions which may tend or draw you to the same, and make speedy return when you shall be sent on your Masters or Mistresses Errands: You shall avoid Idleness, and ever be employed, either in God's Service, or about your Master's Business: You shall be of fair, gentle, and lowly Speech and Behaviour to all Men, and especially to your Governours. And according to your Carriage, expect your Reward, for Good or Ill, from God and your Friends.

1

2

3

4

6

5

3 ENTERTAINMENT BOOK
This volume records the meals provided by the Company and its officers on formal occasions over the period 1637–51. It gives detailed menus and prices and provides a valuable social commentary on the eating habits of the period. At the Master's dinner in 1639 were consumed no less than 32 stones of beef, a sheep, 11 geese, 12 capons, 66 pigeons, 16 quarts of cream and 300 eggs, to select only a few items from those purchased.

The opening shown relates to a dinner provided 'at the Miter Taverne in Fenchurch Streete the 31 of October 1638 [for] the King and Queenes most excellent Majesties and her Majesties most royall mother, the Queene mother of France'. The menu comprised loin and leg of veal, shoulder of mutton, capons, rabbits, oranges, cucumbers, and bread, beer and wine.
Guildhall ms. 22,191

4 WARRANT AUTHORISING A COUNTRY SEARCH
From 1474 until 1702 the Company regularly carried out county-wide searches of the premises of provincial pewterers looking for defective workmanship or sub-standard alloys. Local officials such as justices were required by statute to assist the searchers who carried with them a warrant setting out and authorising their powers. The warrant shown is that for the search of 1682.
Guildhall ms. 22,198/2

5 COUNTRY SEARCH BOOK
The records of the country searches provide much detailed information on provincial pewterers, listing the wares found in their shops, the extent to which the alloy used fell short of the 'assay of London', and the fines levied on them for transgressing the Company's standards. The volume for the years 1669–83 is shown open at the search of Wrexham and Ludlow in 1677.
Guildhall ms. 7105/2

6 RULES OF 1639/40
The Company sought to regulate the price at which its members sold their wares. Detailed lists of prices were produced periodically and these often set out wholesale prices to be charged by one pewterer to another; discounts to be offered to 'country chapmen' who distributed London-made pewter outside the capital, and retail prices to be charged to the public at large. This document is of particular interest as the only one surviving in its original form and which, as such, bears the signatures of some one hundred and twenty London pewterers agreeing to be bound by it. It is of interest that only four 'signed' with a mark, the rest were able to write their names.

Among the wares listed are 'sadware' (plates and dishes in general), long dishes, basins, bowls, cisterns, stoolpans, alembics ('lembicks'), flagons, pottingers and stills. Also included is the fee to be charged for hiring pewterware and the surcharge allowed for granting a purchaser three months and six months credit.
Guildhall ms. 22,202

DARK AGES TO 1400

After the departure of the Romans, the manufacture of pewter either ceased or was at a very low level. When the trade slowly re-asserted itself the pewter made was for a limited market, primarily for religious use. In addition to the few items of flatware or holloware that have survived, a range of small objects are known, used mostly for personal adornment and often associated with religious pilgrimages.

7 CRUCIFIX FIGURE, in the style of c1160–70

The Christ is sadly mutilated, His left arm bent, His right arm and feet broken off and all the surfaces corroded. It is solid cast but some of the finer detail would originally have been applied in paint over a gesso ground (vestiges of red paint are still visible). The loincloth arranged in a bold 'damp-fold' and held by a large knot at the hip suggests parallels with English manuscript illumination of the third quarter of the 12th century and particularly with the Copenhagen Psalter. 5in high (127mm)

British Museum, on loan from the Rector and Parochial Church Council of St. Paul's Ludgvan, Cornwall

Found in the Norman south wall of the chancel at Ludgvan in 1912–13.

LIT. *Sir Eric Maclagan, 'A Crucifix Figure from Ludgvan Church, Cornwall',* ANTIQUARIES JOURNAL, *Vol. XX (1940), p509, pl XCIII; A.H. Hitchens,* LUDGVAN PARISH CHURCH. A SHORT HISTORY, *c1973; Neil Stratford,* ENGLISH ROMANESQUE ART 1066–1200, *Catalogue Hayward Gallery, London 1984, no. 240, p245.*

This is the only surviving Romanesque pewter crucifix (made from 68% tin, 32% lead), not only from the British Isles but from Europe as a whole. There must be every likelihood that the Christ was made locally, bearing unique witness to high-class metalworking in the 12th century close to the tin sources.

8 JEWELLERY, 11th century

Some items from a group of partly-finished beads, brooches and rings. Diam. of largest brooch 1¾in (45mm)
Museum of London, 3904, 3906, 3910, 3912, 3914, 3929, 3945

Found at Cheapside opposite St. Mary-le-Bow church, City of London, in 1838.

The existence of this group of unfinished material appears to confirm that pewter or tin alloy items were being manufactured in London in the late Saxon/Norman period. The largest brooch appears to have been made from the same mould as one found in Viking Dublin in an 11th-12th century context in Christ Church Place (information from B.Ó Ríordáin). Other pewter brooches are known from contexts of a similar date from York and elsewhere.

7

8

9

10

11

9   TOKENS, 13th century
Seven tin-lead tokens
Museum of London, SWA 81 ⟨408⟩, ⟨412⟩,
⟨598⟩, ⟨706⟩, ⟨707⟩, ⟨1984⟩, ⟨2142⟩

Discovered in 1981 by the Department of
Urban Archaeology during excavations at
Swan Lane, City of London.

Tokens in a lead alloy appear to have been
used during the Middle Ages in England as
small change. This group is an example of
the earliest known series.

10   MIRROR CASE, late 13th century
One side of the case decorated with a cross,
circles and diaper ornament.
2⅛ diam (53mm)
Museum of London, 84.240/5

Found at Billingsgate, City of London.

LIT. *J. Bayley, P. Drury and B. Spencer, 'A*
Medieval Mirror from Heybridge, Essex',
ANTIQUARIES JOURNAL *64 (1984) 401,*
p1.LIIIe

Other pewter mirror cases have been found
in Perth and London. They originally contained small convex mirrors backed with
lead.

**11   SEPULCHRAL CHALICE, 14th cen-
tury**
The chalice has a wide cup bowl and simple
knopped stem. Restored on the bowl and
foot.
3½in high (90mm)
Principal private collection

Found during excavations for a croquet lawn
at Stoneleigh Abbey in 1908.

LIT. *P.R.G. Hornsby,* PEWTER OF THE WESTERN
WORLD, *1983, no. 153; J. Pewter Soc., Spring*
1986, for details of three further chalices.

Chalices of a high lead pewter, such as this
example, were frequently buried with priests
from the 11th to the 15th centuries.

12 FLAGON, late 14th century
An octagonal flagon with knopped lid and twin-ball thumbpiece. The body is made from eight strips or panels of pewter; the lid is cast. Worn touchmark under the lid.
9½in high (240mm)
Private collection

Found in the River Medway near Tonbridge Castle, Kent.

EXHIB. AGE OF CHIVALRY, Royal Academy, London, 1987, no 211.

Flagons of this form are also known from Switzerland and France. Two similar examples were excavated from the ruins of Homburg Castle which was destroyed in 1356, thus confirming a 14th century date for the form. Another example has recently been discovered at Bristol and is now in Bristol Museum. As with a number of other early forms the question must remain as to whether all examples were made on the Continent or if some were manufactured in England during the early days of the English pewter industry. There is interesting evidence to suggest that the latter is true. The 1348 Ordinances and the Assay of 1438 (referring to the sizes and weights of English pewter then being made), lists 'square' flagons. In 1455 there is further reference in the Ordinances to square pots which had to be charged at 10*d* for the quart. At that time 'square' meant colloquially a figure with straight sides, rather than a rectangle with four right-angles. In 1482 there is another reference to 'Normandy' pottes, a confirmation that the origins of this style were French but that examples were being made in England. The weight of this example, 2*lb* 10*oz*, is close to the weight listed for a quart potte in the 1438 Assay; it holds 42 fluid ounces, within the tolerance of the contemporary ale standard quart.

12

13 BOWL, 14th century
With edge fillet for strengthening on the upper side of the rim. Crowned hammer mark and single and double ownership marks.
7in diam (180mm)
The Worshipful Company of Pewterers, S1/130

From the Thames foreshore.

One of the earliest bowls or deep saucers known. See also a 14th century example from Exeter, *Allan, p345, fig. 192.* Recent study shows that the earliest plates from archaeological sites have a strengthening edge on the upper side of the rim. Later plates have it below the rim.

LIT. R. Brownsword and E.E.H. Pitt, 'X-Ray Fluorescence Analysis of English 13th-16th Century Pewter Flatware', ARCHAEOMETRY 26, 2 (1984), pp237–44.

13

14

15

14 PLATE, 14th century
The plate has sloping sides and a wide flat central boss. The touch or quality mark is the pewterer's hammer, struck on the rim. The surface is covered with nature's gilding.
11in diam (280mm)
Private collection

Pewter from waterlogged (*ie* anaerobic) situations such as river mud, is usually well preserved, little oxygen having gained contact with the metal. Surfaces are frequently distinguished by the presence of 'nature's gilding' — a golden patination believed to be due to burial in iron-rich deposits.

15 CRUET, 14th century
A six-sided cruet, the cover with hammerhead thumbpiece.
4in high (102mm)
The Earl of Bradford

Found at Tong Castle, Shropshire.

LIT. J. Pewter Society, Spring 1978

Similar to one in the Victoria and Albert Museum, London m.26–1939

16 LID, 14th century
Part of an hexagonal lid from a salt surmounted by the figure of the Virgin and with three relief-cast scenes: part of the Annunciation, the Virgin and Child enthroned, and one of the three Kings. An inscription in Lombardic capitals reads
'[GR]ACIA.P[LENA].DOMINUS.TE:+REX[...]'
(...full of grace, the Lord is with thee).
1¾in high (44mm)
Museum of London 86.105

From the Thames foreshore at Billingsgate, City of London.

LIT. C. Roach Smith 'Cover of a leaden box or cup found in the bed of the Thames', COLLECTANEA ANTIQUA *I, (1848), pp115–22, plXLIII*

A near complete lid of this same form, also from the Thames, is now in the British Museum (M & LA 56 7–1 2175).

16

17 SPOONS
Left to right:
(a) *Round bowled,* 14th century, with narrowing stem and filed knop.
6½in (165mm)
Principal private collection

(b) *Round bowled,* 14th century, with cut knop.
7in (178mm)
Principal private collection

(c) *Knopped,* 13th-14th century, with two balls, iron core.
6¼in (160mm)
Museum of London, 8260

One of the earliest known spoons.

(d) *Latten wrythen knop,* 15th century.
6½in (166mm)
Museum of London, 86.443/2

Excavated from the Thames foreshore, Southwark, London.

18 CANDLESTICK, *c*1400
A candlestick with simple socket, dished base and lightly knopped hollow stem blocked with wax and cotton wick.
4in high (100mm)
Museum of London, 78.238/1

Excavated from the Thames foreshore, Queenhithe, City of London.

LIT. *Museum of London,* PEWTER, *1983, p22*

Copper alloy candlesticks of this style are known to have been used both in France and England during the 14th century. This is the only pewter example to have been found. It has a high lead content as permitted for holloware ('rounded vessels') in the 1348 Ordinances. (Analysis by Dr Roger Brownsword)

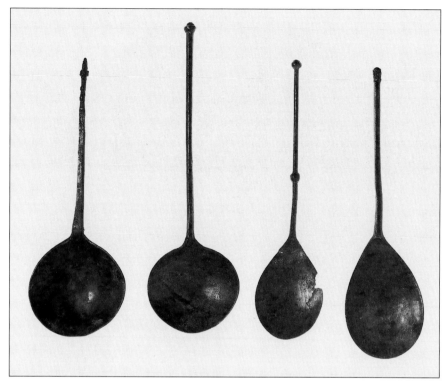

17

18

19

19 MINIATURE UTENSILS, 13th to 16th century
A group of small jugs, ewers or flagons, cast decorated with hatching, ladder patterns, scales and fluting.
2in high (44–51mm).
Private collection

From the Thames foreshore.

Miniatures such as these were cast from stone moulds, one example (of a jug mould) being known from excavations at York. Elaborate cast decoration was used on the hexagonal cruets from Weoley Castle, Birmingham (*Catalogue* no.136) and Ludlow Castle, which date from the 14th century. However, these cruets are approximately three times the size of the 'toys' illustrated here and were intended as functional items at the Mass, for holding wine and water. Other toys are known from the Van Beuningen Museum, Rotterdam and from excavations at Amsterdam, which show the influence of full size ceramic and metal types.

LIT. J.M. Baart et al, OPGRAVINGEN IN AMSTERDAM, *1977; I. Dufour et al,* KEUR VAN TIN UIT DE HAVENSTEDEN AMSTERDAM, ANTWERPEN EN ROTTERDAM, *1979, pp243–6, no.25.*

20 CANDLESTICK, 14th century
A small candlestick on three feet, with cast inscription.
2in high (51mm)
Principal private collection

LIT. J. Pewter Soc., Autumn 1987.

20

21 BADGE, late 14th century
The figure of a woman, perhaps a milkmaid, the legs missing.
2¼in high (57mm)
Museum of London, 88.446

From Southwark Bridge, London

LIT. B. Spencer, forthcoming catalogue of badges in Salisbury Museum.

More complete badges of similar design from London and Salisbury suggest that the figure wore high boots and perhaps held a garland in her right hand. In some cases three flagons or conical measures are balanced on her head. It is suggested that these badges represent milkmaids taking part in Mayday festivities and dancing with garlands and flagons and wearing headdresses made up of metal milk jugs, as they continued to do until the 19th century.

21

15th AND 16th CENTURIES

The pewter industry evolved slowly to meet the demand for domestic and institutional pewter. At first pewter remained very much a luxury, but by the 16th century its role had widened and pewter was to be found at most levels of society, except the indigent poor. The range of objects made also expanded.

22   BADGE, 15th century
A badge with six acorn-knopped spoons in a bowl.
1⅞in high (48mm)
Museum of London, 86.202/43

From Bankside, Southwark.

23   LIVERY BADGE, 15th century
Five arrows bound together by a belt. Left in its rough unfinished state.
2⅜in high (60mm)
Museum of London, 82.8/16

From Bull Wharf, City of London.

This emblem was adopted by John of Gaunt in the 14th century and by Prince Arthur in the 15th century.

24   NEEDLECASE, 15th century
An octagonal needlecase with twin lugs for suspension. Inscribed in black letters MATER DEI MEMENTO (Mother of God remember me) with a further garbled line and similarly on the other side IASPAR MELCHIOR BAL (the names of the three kings, the last, Balthazar, being incomplete), with a further unclear line. On the base there is a relief cast Agnus Dei and the lid has two lily pots and scrollwork.
3⅝ long (93mm)
Museum of London, 86.202/2

From Bull Wharf, City of London.

25   MINIATURE FLAGON, 16th century
A pear-shaped miniature flagon, with pin and lid missing.
2in high (51mm)
Private collection

From the Thames foreshore.

Full sized wine flagons of this shape are known on the Continent from the 14th century but were also made by English pewterers until the early 17th century. A similar, but full sized, flagon from the *Mary Rose* is the earliest extant example in this country. The earliest known illustration of vessels of this form is the pottle (or potel, ½gallon measure) in the Exchequer Standard of 1496 (see p37).

22

24

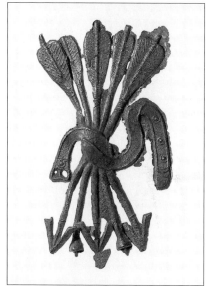

23

25

28

29

26

Detail of 27

27

26 FIGURINE, c1600
A male figurine, hollow-cast but lacking his hat.
3in high (76mm)
Museum of London, 88.9/35

From the Thames foreshore.

LIT. H. Nickel, 'The Little Knights of the living room table' METROPOLITAN MUSEUM OF ART BULLETIN *25, No. 4 (1966), p175, fig. 13.*

At least four other male figures are known from the same provenance but they come from different moulds, also a contemporary female figure. A few two-dimensional or flat male and female figures of the same date are also known. The looped hands suggest that children danced these figures across a table on a piece of string.

27 PRINCE OF WALES PLATE, c1485
A plate with sloping sides, deep bowl and central boss. Stamped on the rim is an ostrich feather, the emblem of the Prince of Wales.
10½in diam (267mm)
Principal private collection

One of a small hoard of flatware excavated during work at Guy's Hospital, London, in 1899.

EXHIB. Clifford's Inn Hall, 1908, no. 31; Reading Museum, 1969, nos. 11–13; PEWTERWARE WITH ROYAL ASSOCIATIONS, *Pewterers' Hall, London, 1974, nos. 2–3.*

LIT. Plates from the hoard have been illustrated and discussed in several books, including: R.F. Michaelis, ANTIQUE PEWTER OF THE BRITISH ISLES, *1955, fig. 18; Museum of London (1983), p13; C.A. Peal,* BRITISH PEWTER, *1971, fig. 24.*

The plates have been attributed to the household of Arthur, Prince of Wales, who died in 1502.

28 SAUCER, c1500
A broad-rimmed saucer with deep bowl and central boss. Marked with owner's initials 'S' and crowned 'I'.
5¾in diam (148mm)
Museum of London, A419

Found at Westminster.

LIT. Museum of London (1983), p14.

29 BROAD-RIMMED SAUCER, c1500
A broad-rimmed saucer with 'nature's gilding'. With letter 'W' struck on rim.
7¼in diam (184mm)
Principal private collection

LIT. P.R.G. Hornsby, PEWTER, COPPER AND BRASS, *1981, fig. 22.*

30   PORRINGER, 1500–50
A small bowl-shaped porringer with solid trefoil ear or handle. Initials 'IB' stamped on the
ear. Touchmark of a star with a 'T' in base.
5¼in diam (134mm)
Principal private collection

LIT. R.F. Michaelis, ENGLISH PEWTER
PORRINGERS, *Apollo, July to Sept. 1949.*

Two-eared porringers of tri-lobed form were
found on the *Mary Rose* and therefore date
before 1545.
   Porringers were used for everyday eating
of soft foods, such as soups, gruels, stews
and porridges.

31   PORRINGER, c1550
A deep-bowled porringer with open trefoil
ear. Initials 'IFC' on bowl.
4½in diam (114mm)
Principal private collection

Found in the Thames, near Hampton Court.

32   PORRINGER, 16th century
A deep porringer with two fleur-de-lys
shaped ears. The touchmark incorporates
'IH' with a merchant's mark.
7¼in diam (185mm)
Museum of London, 8130

30

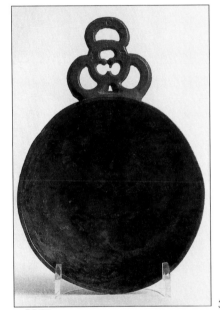

31

32

33   SPOONS WITH FIGURE KNOPS
Left to right:
(a) *Jester,* 15th century
6in (152mm)
Museum of London, 83.349

From the Thames foreshore.

The only known example of this knop.

(b) ***Horned headdress,*** 15th century, touch-mark a cross.
6½in (165mm)
Museum of London, 28.112/14

(c) ***Lion Sejant,*** 16th century, touchmark 'TF' in bowl
6½in (165mm)
Principal private collection

LIT. R.F. Homer, FIVE CENTURIES OF BASE METAL SPOONS, 1975, p35.

(d) ***Maidenhead,*** *c*1500, with cross mark in bowl
6½in (165mm)
Principal private collection

(e) ***Apostle,*** *c*1500, with touchmark of a key and initials 'RI'. Owner's initial 'D' in bowl.
7in (178mm)
Principal private collection

(f) ***Alderman knop,*** *c*1500, daisy mark in bowl.
6½in (165mm)
Principal private collection

LIT. Homer (1975), p26.

Pewter spoons tended to follow the forms made popular in silver and in latten (a form of brass), although there are some knops unique to pewter, including the horned headdress.

33

34 SPOONS WITH GEOMETRIC KNOPS
Left to right:

(a) **Stump End,** *c*1600, touchmark a crowned rose.
6¼in (160mm)
Museum of London, 12339

(b) **Baluster knop,** 16th century with cross mark and initials 'TP'.
6¼in (160mm)
Principal private collection

(c) **Hexagonal knop,** *c*1600, with touch-mark 'IF'.
6¼in (160mm)
Principal private collection

(d) **Acorn knop,** 16th century with touch-mark of lion and 'H' in bowl.
5½in (140mm)
Principal private collection

(e) **Denticulated ball or melon knop,** 16th century with worn touchmarks.
6¾in (172mm)
Principal private collection

(f) **Diamond point,** 15th century
6½in (165mm)
Principal private collection

34

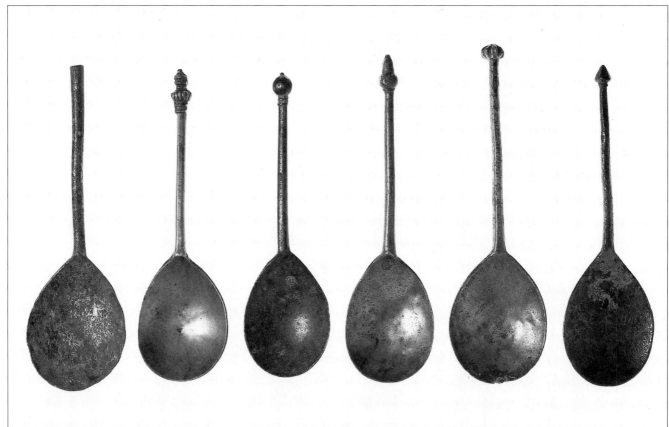

35

36

37

35   FLASK, mid-16th century
Bulbous flask with two handles for a strap, left-hand threaded screw top; for drugs or spirits.
4½in high (115mm)
Museum of London, A23216

From Cannon Street, City of London.

A series of similar flasks were found in the barber-surgeon's cabin on the *Mary Rose.* See Margaret Rule, THE MARY ROSE, 1982, pp186–96.

36   PLATE, 16th century
A plate with sloping sides and central boss, the rim decorated with cast 'chatter' marks.
11¾in diam (300mm)
Principal private collection

Found at Boston, Lincolnshire.

37   THREE PLATES, 16th century
A set of three plates with plain rim and sloping booge. By 'IP'.
6in, 9½in and 12¼in diam (153mm, 242mm and 312mm)
Principal private collection

Excavated at Witham on the Hill, Lincolnshire.

EXHIB. *Usher Gallery, Lincoln, 1962, no. 244; Reading Museum, 1969, nos. 23–25.* LIT. H.H. Cotterell, OLD PEWTER, ITS MAKERS AND MARKS, *1929, pl LId.*

This type of plate, known as a 'Spanish trencher', could be exported without first being beaten in the booge to strengthen it.

38   DISH, c1600
A large dish or bowl with sloping sides and slight central boss. Owners' initials 'WMF' struck on the rim, with a touchmark of a crown over 'IB' and the date 1594 on the reverse.
16½in diam (420mm)
Private collection

Few pewter dishes and chargers of this size have survived from this period. This is the earliest recorded dated English touchmark.

39   THURDENDALE, c1575–1610
A measure with hooped body, tapering sides, strap handle and slightly rounded lid, wedge and lens thumbpiece. Made by 'SC', the mark with a daisy.'HR' capacity mark on the lid, confirming that it was of approved capacity.
8¾in high (222mm)
Private collection

LIT. *C.A. Peal*, PEWTER OF GREAT BRITAIN, *1983, p50; J. Pewter Soc., Autumn 1976.*

The capacity of this measure is 45 fluid ounces. Banded measures also occur in the late 17th century but the construction and thumbpiece of this example suggest that it is of an earlier date. The exact definition of a thurdendale is uncertain. However during the 17th century there is evidence that thurdendales were being made to the quart ale standard, the additional 5 fluid ounces being designed to take the froth or head of ale. It is interesting to note that the capacity of this example is also one-third of a wine gallon.

38

39

40 BULBOUS FLAGON, c1500
Bulbous flagon with twin ball thumbpiece,
strap handle, the lid with a central boss.
8in high (203mm)
Principal private collection

Found in the Thames at Deptford in 1908.

LIT. *Peal (1971), fig. 21.*

41 FLAGON, 16th century
A pear-shaped or bulbous flagon with narrow
stem, rounded lid with twin ball thumbpiece.
Inside the lid is a copper medallion with
stamped fleur-de-lys. Scratch date of 1620
under foot.
11½in high (292mm)
Principal private collection

LIT. *Hornsby (1983), no. 701; Exhibition
catalogue,* ENGLAND AT THE TIME OF THE
ARMADA, *Grosvenor House, 1988, no. 26.*

A very similar flagon was found in the *Mary
Rose,* illustrated in Peal, *Pewter of Great Britain,* no. 3.

41

40

42 FLAGON, c1590–1610
A bulbous flagon with knopped lid, pear-shaped body, 'S' shaped handle and trefoil thumbpiece. Traces of a touchmark on the back of the thumbpiece.
12½in high (173mm)
The Worshipful Company of Pewterers, S2/213

Formerly in the Church of Holy Rood, Woodeaton, Oxfordshire.

EXHIB. *Reading Museum, 1969, no. 30*

LIT. *A.V. Sutherland Graeme, 'Pewter Church Flagons',* CONNOISSEUR, *June 1946; R.F. Michaelis, 'Pear-shaped Pewter Flagons',* ANTIQUE COLLECTOR, *Oct. 1961; and J. Pewter Soc., Autumn 1981, for a discussion on these flagons. See also Worshipful Company of Pewterers,* CATALOGUE, *1968 and 1979; Michaelis (1955), fig. 60; R.F. Michaelis,* BRITISH PEWTER, *1969, p17.*

A flagon of this form appears with a James I flagon in the mark of 'EG' a noted flagon maker of the early Stuart period. Flagons of this general form are also recorded on the Continent but date from an earlier period. It is never possible to state with absolute certainty whether a particular example is of English or Continental origin. New evidence, published here for the first time, reveals that the earliest English dated illustration of a vessel of this form is included in the Exchequer Standard of 1496, so providing it with an official English identity, (see no.25). It seems likely, because of its provenance as well as the use of a flagon of this shape in a contemporary English mark, that this and nos. 43 and 44 are English.

42

43

43 SPOUTED FLAGON, c1600

A bulbous flagon with 'S' shaped handle, rounded knopped lid, narrow stem and stepped foot; the spout with small cover. Touchmark of a lion passant in a beaded circle on the thumbpiece.
11½in high (292mm)
Principal private collection

LIT. *Hornsby (1983), no. 744.*

Spouted flagons are known in English silver and the general style is also found on Continental flagons. There are two similar pewter flagons in the Byloke Museum, Ghent, by Edward Glover, an English pewterer. The outline body form should be compared with nos. 42 and 44.

44 BULBOUS FLAGON, c1580–1620

A rounded or bulbous spouted flagon with 'S' shaped handle, rounded lid and lens type thumbpiece. Worn touchmarks on handle.
13½in high (343mm)
Principal private collection

LIT. *R.F. Michaelis, 'Pear-shaped Pewter Flagons',* ANTIQUE COLLECTOR, *October, 1961.*

44

45 'BELL' CANDLESTICK, c1580–1620
A bell-shaped candlestick with mid drip tray
and baluster knopped stem.
8¼in high (210mm)
Principal private collection

EXHIB. *Usher Gallery, Lincoln, 1962, no. 15;
Reading Museum, 1969, no. 34.*

LIT. *Hornsby (1983); no. 1060; Michaelis,
1969, p71; R.F. Michaelis,* OLD DOMESTIC BASE
METAL CANDLESTICKS, *1969, fig. 90; Peal
(1971), p90.*

A few similar candlesticks are known which
date from the late 16th century, but it seems
likely that the style did continue into the
17th century.

45

46

17th CENTURY

The pewter industry developed rapidly in the 17th century and achieved its greatest prosperity after the Restoration of Charles II in 1660. A whole range of domestic pewter found its way into the homes of most classes of society. Dishes, chargers, plates and saucers were the most popular items but spoons, candlesticks and salts were also commonly to be found.

46 'JAMES I' FLAGON, c1610–20
Slightly tapering body with 'S' shaped handle and solid erect thumbpiece. Trace of a mark on the handle.
17¾in high (450mm)
Principal private collection

LIT. *J. Pewter Soc., Autumn 1981.*

Flagons of this form were almost certainly in use domestically prior to 1600 and it was this form which was immediately adopted throughout England after the Church in 1603 allowed the use of pewter at the communion. Examples with churchwarden's initials or other inscriptions can be presumed to be ecclesiastical, but other plain flagons may well have been used in the home. This is the largest recorded James I flagon.

47 'CHARLES I' FLAGON, c1630–40
A slightly tapering flagon with knopped rounded lid, stepped foot and bar-and-heart thumbpiece. Ownership initials 'SHIN'
10¼in high (260mm)
Principal private collection

This style of flagon gradually replaced the 'James I', although the two forms may well have been made concurrently.

48 'BEEFEATER' FLAGON, c1660
With straight-sided body, flat lid and twin-cusp thumbpiece.
12in high (305mm)
Principal private collection

LIT. *J. Pewter Soc., Spring 1986.*

This style of flagon evolved towards the end of the first half of the 17th century. It is termed a 'beefeater' because of a similarity between the lid and the cap of the Yeomen Warders at the Tower of London.

47

48

49 FLAGON, mid-17th century
A 'beefeater' flagon with slightly curved lid, typical twin-cusp thumbpiece but with a very wide base. Touchmark of 'IB' in a beaded circle struck in the base.
9½in high (242mm)
The Worshipful Company of Pewterers, S2/207

LIT. *Pewterers' Company (1968/79); Hornsby (1983), no. 650; Peal (1983), no. 8.*

There has been some speculation as to the reasons for the very wide base found on this and a few similar flagons. Could they have been designed for use at sea?

50 FLAGON, c1699
Another form of the 'beefeater' flagon, made by John Emes of London. Inscribed 'IHS' and IN USUM ECCLES PAR DE BAGINGTON IN COR WAR 1699.
11¾in high (292mm)
The Worshipful Company of Pewterers, S2/204

LIT. *Pewterers' Company, (1968/79).*

Emes and his son are thought to have been the only makers of this exact style of flagon. Note the curved lid, hammering on the body and the stepped base.

49

50

Detail of 50

51

52

51   CANDLESTICK, c1590–1620
A candlestick with mid drip pan, ribbed stem and rounded base.
9in high (230mm)
Principal private collection

The only known example of its type.

52   BALL-KNOPPED   CANDLESTICK, c1640
A large 'ball' candlestick with dished base, separate sconce. The touchmark includes the initials 'RC' and the date 1636. Owner's initials 'MB'.
8in high (203mm)
Principal private collection

LIT. *J. Pewter Soc., Autumn 1981 and Autumn 1983; Hornsby (1983), cover.*

Until recently this form of candlestick had been dated to around 1670–90, but new evidence suggests that what were termed 'bawle' candlesticks were common around 1600.

53   CANDLESTICK, c1660–80
A typical 'trumpet-based' candlestick, with
mid drip pan. This example has a brass fillet
or band round the foot, either to strengthen it
or as a selling feature.
6¼in high (158mm)
Principal private collection

LIT. *Hornsby (1983), no. 89.*

The name given to this style of candlestick
relates to their similarity in shape to a trumpet and has no other significance. The drip
pan was used to catch the melting wax.

**54   PAIR OF 'TRUMPET-BASED'
CANDLESTICKS, mid-17th century**
Pair of candlesticks with plain drip tray, ribbed stems and loose sconces. The sconces
and bases are engraved with an unidentified
coat-of-arms and stamped with maker's hallmarks; there is also a worn touchmark on the
top of each stem.
9¼in high (235mm)
*The Worshipful Company of Pewterers, S6/
600.1–2*

LIT. *Pewterers' Company (1968/79);
Hornsby (1983), no. 1060.*

Pewter examples of this style are rare but
similar brass candlesticks are more common
and are thought to date from around 1650–
1710.

55   CANDLESTICK, mid 17th-century
A plain stemmed trumpet-based candlestick,
with turned stem and wide foot, by 'RB';
initialled 'CRE' on base.
6¼in high (160mm)
Principal private collection

LIT. *Hornsby (1981); Hornsby (1983), no.
1062; Peal (1983), no. 63.*

The more common forms of trumpet-based
candlesticks are shown as nos. 53 and 54.
This is the only recorded example of this
form of candlestick without a drip tray;
however, similar brass examples are known.

54

53

55

56 OCTAGONAL CANDLESTICK, c1670–80
A typical candlestick with octagonal base and sconce but with round drip pan; the stem decorated with fillets and the tray and foot cast with rope-work decoration. Worn touchmark, initials 'BY' on foot.
7¼in high (184mm)
Principal private collection

There are a number of candlesticks of this basic form, each of slightly different design. They are generally dated to after the Restoration of Charles II.

57 OCTAGONAL CANDLESTICK, c1670
An octagonal candlestick with ribbed stem and initialled 'ED'.
6¼in high (160mm)
Principal private collection

LIT. *Michaelis (1978), fig. 130.*

58 OCTAGONAL CANDLESTICK, c1670
With eight-sided sconce, drip tray and foot, the stem ribbed. By 'IF'; owner's initials 'MB'.
9in high (230mm)
Principal private collection

56

57

58

**59 HEXAGONAL CANDLESTICK,
second half 17th century**
An hexagonal based candlestick with fluted
drip tray in the form of a six-pointed star,
baluster and ball stem.
9¾in high (245mm)
The Worshipful Company of Pewterers,
S6/ 602

LIT. *Pewterers' Company (1968/79).*

60   PAIR OF TAPERSTICKS, c1650–75
A pair of octagonal based taper candlesticks,
with similarly shaped drip pans and candle
sconces.
4¼in high (108mm)
Principal private collection

EXHIB. *Usher Gallery, Lincoln, 1962, no.9*

LIT. *Michaelis (1955), fig. 48; Michaelis
(1978), fig. 130.*

In essence tapersticks are simply small
candlesticks. They were used in a variety of
ways: for occasions when only a little light
was required, in conjunction with stan-
dishes and writing desks where they were
also employed for sealing letters, and for taking a light from one part of the home to
another.

59

60

61

61   PAIR OF TAPERSTICKS, c1680
A pair of square-based taper candlesticks, with square drip trays and ribbed stems.
2¼in high (57mm)
Principal private collection

62   PAIR OF BALL-KNOPPED CANDLE-STICKS, c1690
A pair of candlesticks with wrythen ball knops on the stem and fluted rectangular bases.
6½in high (165mm)
Principal private collection

63   BALL-KNOPPED   CANDLESTICK, c1680–90
Ball-knopped candlestick with round base and ridged ball.
6in high (152mm)
Principal private collection

LIT. *Hornsby (1981), no.49.*

62

63

64   OCTAGONAL SAUCER, c1670
Unusual saucer with rope-work cast border, by 'IL'.
5in diam (127mm).
Principal private collection

Compare this saucer with the top of the master salt (no. 65). It is known that pewterers made use of their moulds to make parts for more than one item.

65   MASTER SALT, c1670–80
An octagonal salt with rope-twist cast decoration on bowl and foot and with cast vines and fruit at the middle of the base.
3in (76mm)
Principal private collection

EXHIB. *Reading Museum, 1969, no. 130.*

LIT. *J. Pewter Soc., Spring 1980.*

The term 'master' is a reference both to the size of such salts and the possible restriction in their use to the people at the top or head of the table.

66   CAPSTAN SALT, c1680–90
A salt with gadrooned top and base.
2¼in wide (56mm)
Principal private collection

67   TRENCHER SALT, c1680–1710
Small salt with dished bowl, by 'IH'.
1½in high (36mm)
Private collection

LIT. *Hornsby (1983), no.393.*

64

65

66

67

70

Detail of 70

68

69

68 MINIATURE BELL, 17th century
Cast decorated with the initials 'IDQ'.
1¼in high (30mm)
Museum of London, 81.49

From the Thames foreshore.

LIT. Ivor Noel Hume, A GUIDE TO ARTIFACTS OF COLONIAL AMERICA, 1978, pp313–21; J.M. Baart, OPGRAVINGEN IN AMSTERDAM, 1977, pp466–71; A.J. Van der Horst, 'De Speelgoodhorloges Van Vlooienburg', ANTIEK, 20/1, 1985, pp28–31; G. Fairclough, PLYMOUTH EXCAVATIONS: ST ANDREW'S STREET 1976 (Plymouth Museum Archaeology Series 2, 1979), pp127–8; P. Saunders, CHANNELS TO THE PAST: THE SALISBURY DRAINAGE COLLECTION, Salisbury and South Wiltshire Museum, 1986.

A small decorated panel by the same maker, dated 1640, also exists and toys bearing the initials 'IDQ' have been found in Amsterdam. Toy watches by Hux of London have also been excavated in Amsterdam, indicating some of the difficulties of attributing a country of origin to such pieces. See loving cup by Hux *Catalogue* no. 115.

69 STREET TRADER, late 17th century
A figure with wild fowl and rabbits. Traces of original red paint.
3in high (78mm)
Museum of London, 85.586

From the Thames foreshore.

The depiction of street traders was familiar from medieval times (see milkmaid, no. 21). Street traders each had a particular cry, handed down by custom, which identified them. Illustrations of these cries are known as the 'Cries of London'. This example appears to be influenced by the work of Marcellus Lauron, c1687. (See Pierce Tempest, *The Cryes of the City of London*, 1711).

70 APOTHECARY MEASURE, early 17th century
An apothecary's measure, with two different capacities of ½ fl.oz (16ml) and 1 fl.oz (32ml). Touchmark a bird and initials 'LS'
2in high (53mm)
Museum of London, 82.7

From the Thames foreshore.

LIT. L.G. Mathews, ANTIQUES OF THE PHARMACY, 1971; J. Pewter Soc., Autumn 1978, pp14–18.

This is the earliest known apothecary measure. The same form was used in the 19th century for spirit measures.

71 FEEDING BOTTLE, early 17th century
A pear-shaped feeding bottle with two incised lines on body and screw top. Touchmark 'EW' and date 1611.
6¼in high (158mm)
Museum of London, 88.7

From the Thames foreshore.

LIT. *G.F. Still*, THE HISTORY OF PAEDIATRICS,
THE PROGRESS OF THE STUDY OF DISEASES OF
CHILDREN UP TO THE END OF THE XVIIITH
CENTURY, *1931; J. Pewter Soc., Spring 1979,
pp2–3.*

This is one of the earliest pewter feeding
bottles.

72 SPICE POT, late 17th century
A canister-shaped spice pot with slip-on lid.
4in high (102mm)
Principal private collection

EXHIB. *Currier Gallery, New Hampshire,
1974, no. 158.*

LIT. *Hornsby (1983), no. 417.*

Detail of 71

71

72

73 SPOONS, 17th century
Left to right:
(a) **Tryfid,** cast with Queen Anne portrait and initials 'SS' on back of stem, lace-back decoration on back of the bowl.
7in (180mm)
Private collection

(b) **Tryfid,** with lace-back bowl.
7½in (190mm)
Principal private collection

(c) **Tryfid,** by 'IP'
7in (178mm)
Museum of London, 28.112/5
A latten spoon with two coats of tinning for safe use. Pewter tryfid spoons are also common.

(d) **Puritan,** by 'WL', dated 1668 in the touch.
7¼in (183mm)
Museum of London, A3280

Found in Maze Pond, Guy's Hospital, Southwark.

(e) **Seal top,** with touchmark 'HB'
6in (154mm)
Museum of London, A529

(f) **Slip top,** by 'RA', the mark with two keys; initials 'KE'.
6¾in (170mm)
Principal private collection

From Westminster.

73

74   PORRINGER, c1625
A flat based stepped bowl; the round ear with
small central aperture and decorated with
rope-work and five petals, with the initials
'ID' within. Four hallmarks on the outside of
the bowl.
6¼in wide (160mm)
Principal private collection

75   PORRINGER, c1670
A porringer with rounded bowl and booge
and 'Old English' style ear. Owner's initials
'MG' on the ear. By 'SB', the mark struck in
the bowl.
4¾in diam (120mm)
Principal private collection

76   PORRINGER, c1650–80
With rounded sides or booge. Owner's initials 'DG' scratched on the back of the ear
and touchmark 'RS'
4⅞in diam (123mm)
*The Worshipful Company of Pewterers,
S5/ 501.24*

LIT.*Pewterers' Company (1968/79).*

This is a typical 17th century porringer. A
variety of ears or handles can be found on
this basic shape; this example has a fine
'dolphin' ear.

74

Detail of 74

75

76

77

77 COMMEMORATIVE PORRINGER, c1702

A commemorative porringer with rounded body and decorated ear, with initials 'AR' for Queen Anne. Unidentified touchmark on back of ear.
4⅞in diam (120mm)
The Worshipful Company of Pewterers, S5/ 501.23

LIT. *Pewterers' Company (1968/79); Hornsby (1983), no. 454.*

78 TAZZA, c1685–95

A footed plate or tazza with gadrooned rim and foot. Initials 'RH' and worn touchmark on plate.
9in diam (228mm)
Principal private collection

Plates of this style were used at the Communion, but also found a domestic role for serving sweetmeats and gingerbread.

78

79 PLATE, c1675
A broad-rimmed plate with incised rim, by
James Taudin. An engraved coat-of-arms
within mantling on the rim.
10in diam (254mm)
The Worshipful Company of Pewterers, 41

LIT. *Pewterers' Company (1968/79).*

Taudin, a Huguenot pewterer who worked
in London from the 1650s, introduced the
use of hard metal pewter, which included
antimony.

**80 BROAD-RIMMED PLATE AND
CHARGER, c1670–80**
With contemporary armorials. The plate
with four lion rampant hallmarks struck on
the rim (not illustrated). The charger by
another maker, with four eagle hallmarks.
9¾in and 21½in diam (248mm and
546mm)
Principal private collection

**81 NARROW-RIMMED CHARGER,
c1680**
The surface hammered all over for decoration, by John Kenton.
22in (560mm)
Frank Holt collection

79

80

81

82

83

Detail of 84

82 TRIPLE-REEDED PLATE, late 17th century
One of a set of four triple-reeded plates, by William Howard of Drury Lane, London. Owners' initials 'RTM' struck on rim.
9in diam (230mm)
Private collection

The earliest triple-reeded dishes and plates had incised reeds cut on the wheel, but by 1680 the reeding was part of the mould. The style was popular around 1670 to 1710.

83 PLAIN-RIMMED PLATE, c1695
A plain-rimmed plate, by Erasmus Dole of Bristol. With owner's initials 'MT'.
9¾in diam (248mm)
Private collection

84 BOWL, early 17th century
Bearing the initials 'ID' inside the lip. Apparently unrecorded touchmark 'SI' and the date '38' below (see illustration). The capacity is c700 ml.
6¼in diam (160mm)
Museum of London, 87.41

From the Thames foreshore.

LIT. *MS 7105/2, cat. no.5 for reference to beer bowls in the Company's search of 1677 in Ludlow.*

The Pewterers' Company lists of wares in the 17th century do not include basins weighing less than 1*lb* each. This bowl weighs 359*gm* (12⅔ *oz*). In 1612/13 'small beere bowls' were to weigh 4*lb* 10*oz* per half dozen (12⅓*oz* each). Is this the first 'small beere bowl' to be recognised?

84

85   BOWL, early 17th century
A bowl weighing 242.41*gm* (8.55*oz*). Touch-mark 'WM' and male profile to left.
6¼in diam (160mm)
Museum of London, 87.127/17

From the Thames foreshore.

86   CUP, mid-17th century
With a gadrooned base, probably now lacking a handle.
1¾in high (44mm)
Museum of London, A16573

From Moorfields, City of London.

LIT. Museum of London (1983), p19.

87   TUMBLER CUP, c1680
A round tumbler cup with wrigglework decoration of a grotesque bird and a touchmark incorporating the initials 'IW' dated 1677.
1¾in high (48mm)
Museum of London, A24743

Found at Whitechapel, London.

LIT.Museum of London (1983), p19.

88   POSSETT OR CAUDLE CUP, c1650
A bulbous cup with solid 'S' shaped handle and thumbpiece.
2in high (50mm)
Museum of London, 8176

Found at Moorfields, London.

LIT. Museum of London (1983), p19.

85

Detail of 85

86   87   88

89

91

89 TWO-HANDLED CUP, c1695
A cup with two solid 'S' handles with thumb-pieces. The body decorated with wriggle-work portrait of William III with the initials 'WR'. The touchmark 'CI' in beaded circle.
2¾in high (70mm)
Museum of London, 8175

LIT. *Museum of London (1983), p21.*

90 CAUDLE CUP, c1690
A rare small cup with wrythen or fluted lower half. The handle has a small thumb grip at the top.
2¾in high (70mm)
The Worshipful Company of Pewterers, S3/ 313

LIT. *Pewterers' Company (1968/79); Hornsby (1983), no. 1018.*

Caudle was a sweetened and spiced hot drink made from ale or wine.

91 TAVERN MUG, mid-17th century
A lidless mug of quart capacity with twin incised bands and solid handle. The drum inscribed 'Iohn Kennett in Sheirness Fort suttler 1669'. Touchmark in base of a bird between initials 'WC' and date 164(?).
6¾in high (174mm)
Museum of London, 78.132

From the Thames foreshore.

LIT. *Museum of London (1983), p5; Rosemary Weinstein, 'A London Tankard and The Dutch Wars', TRANSACTIONS OF THE LONDON AND MIDDLESEX ARCHAEOL. SOC., Vol 32 (1981), pp151–2.*

This is one of the earliest dated London pewter tavern pots. The small fort at Sheerness was begun in April 1666 as a defence during the second Dutch war (1664–7). A sutler was responsible for provisions.

90

92 TWO-BANDED TAVERN MUG, c1670–80

A lidless tavern pot of quart ale capacity, by James Donne, inscribed 'John French, Fleet Street, Sohofields'. Owner's initials 'FE' on handle.
6in high (152mm)
Principal private collection

EXHIB. *Reading Museum, 1969, no. 120.*

LIT. *Peal (1983), fig. 69; Michaelis (1955), fig. 30.*

93 TWO-BANDED POT OR MUG, c1680

A two-banded quart capacity ale mug, by 'WV', an unrecorded maker. With crowned 'C' capacity mark for Charles II. Inscribed 'A Winchester Quart exact to the standard at Guildhall'.
6½in high (167mm)
Principal private collection

92

93

94

94 SQUAT MUG, late 17th century

A rare half-pint mug with two raised bands of decoration. The touchmark of 'AW' with three roses in the base. Initials 'ACS' on handle.
3in high (78mm)
Museum of London, A2357

From Smithfield, City of London.

95 TAVERN MUG, c1700

A pint ale mug, by Edward Ubly. With William III capacity marks.
5in high (127mm)
Principal private collection

EXHIB. Reading Museum, 1969, no. 150.

The only tavern mug of this style recorded of pint capacity.

96 TAVERN MUG, c1705

A mug with high fillet, engraved 'Walter Barden att ye Hole in ye Wall in Pearle St Near king street Wapping 1706' and again 'Stop Thife'. Former owners' initials 'WES' on body and marked 'EM' in a diamond.
4¾in high (122mm)
Museum of London, A16808

LIT. Museum of London (1983), p6

96

95

97   FLAT-LIDDED TANKARD, c1650–75
An early flat-lid tankard with squat straight-sided body. The lid has a slightly raised platform with a cast medallion set at the centre. The twin-cusp thumbpiece is more usually found on 'beefeater' flagons. Unidentified touchmark of a man on a horse with initials 'GG'.
4in high to lip (102mm)
The Worshipful Company of Pewterers, S3/307

LIT. *Pewterers' Company (1968/79); Peal (1983), no. 9.*

This example is thought to be one of the earlier flat-lidded tankards. Tankards of this basic form are often engraved with wriggle-work decoration and were popular from 1650 until 1710.

98   FLAT-LIDDED TANKARD, c1670–90
With plain undecorated body and spray thumbpiece. Four hallmarks on the lid, by 'IB'. Owners' initials 'HWA'.
7in high (178mm)
Principal private collection

99   TANKARD, c1695
A straight-sided tankard with domed lid and denticulated rim to lid, by William Eddon.
6¼in high (160mm)
Principal private collection

97

99

98

100

BALUSTER MEASURES

The term 'baluster' is derived from the form of these measures. Pewter measures were used from the 15th century in taverns and within the home. The first, very rare, examples were squat and rounded but by the 16th century tall elongated examples appeared; the style probably derived from pottery vessels and leather blackjacks which were used for much the same purposes. By the 17th century balusters had once more become slightly squatter and this style remained in general use well into the 18th century. The main differences between balusters after 1600 is found in the type of thumbpiece employed. The main forms have been called the 'hammerhead', 'ball', and 'bud' and in the 18th century the 'double volute' and 'spray'. Baluster measures were made from a low quality pewter and contained more lead than was normal. Most have capacity check marks stamped on the neck or lid.

Balusters were used in taverns as measures for wine or spirits. Some may have been drunk from, although the fact that balusters of a gallon downwards were common suggests that some were used for the sale of wine or ale, which was then poured into a cup or mug of pewter, leather, wood or pottery. Until 1826 two national systems of capacity were in use in England: the wine pint being smaller than the ale pint.

100   MEASURE, before 1545
Of typical baluster form, with apparently unique flat 'plume' thumbpiece.
5⅞ in high (150mm)
The Mary Rose Trust MR81 A651

Recovered from Henry VIII's warship *Mary Rose* which sank off Portsmouth in 1545.

LIT. *Rule (1982)*

This measure is similar in shape to wine measures which continued in use (with subtle changes of form) until the late 18th century. See nos.101–105.

101   BALUSTER MEASURE, 16th century
A tall and thin baluster with ball thumbpiece, of quart capacity with 'hR' capacity
mark. The lid and base have several house-
marks including three birds, possibly cranes,
a merchant's mark and the initials 'TP'; there
is also a touchmark of 'I' in a circle.
8½in high (215mm)
Museum of London, 80.227

Found at Three Cranes Wharf, on the
Thames foreshore.

LIT. *Museum of London (1983), p9.*

**102   'HAMMERHEAD' BALUSTER
MEASURE, c1675**
A rare pint capacity baluster measure, with
'hammerhead' thumbpiece.
7in high (178mm)
Principal private collection

LIT. *Hornsby (1981), fig. 41; Hornsby
(1983), no. 812.*

The thumbpiece is known as a 'hammerhead' from its similarity to that tool.

102

101

Detail of 101

103 'BALL' BALUSTER MEASURE, late 17th century

Pint capacity, the lid with rare locating flange underneath the lid. Initialled 'RA'.
7in high (178mm)
Principal private collection

LIT. *Hornsby (1981), fig. 41; Hornsby (1983), no. 813.*

The 'ball' thumbpiece was in use at the same time as the 'hammerhead' and 'bud' during the 17th century.

104 'BUD' BALUSTER MEASURE, c1685

Pint capacity baluster measure with 'bud' thumbpiece, by Thomas Battison, London. The touchmark and capacity mark 'HR' are stamped on the neck, or collar, of the measure.
6½in high (165mm)
Private collection

This form of thumbpiece evolved in the 17th century and went out of fashion in the early 18th century.

105 GALLON AND HALF-GALLON BALUSTER MEASURES, 17th century

Both with 'bud' thumbpieces. The half-gallon by A. Banckes.
13in and 10¾in high (330mm and 273mm)
Principal private collection

The gallon was found at Kingshill house, Swindon, in 1890.

104

103

105

CORPORATION PEWTER

The following pieces are of interest because they have associations with the corporate life of the City. No. 108 was made by a pewterer who became Lord Mayor; the other three pieces bear the arms of Livery Companies.

106 CAST DECORATED WINE CUP, c1610–20

A long-stemmed footed cup with relief cast decoration. The bowl has four roundels alternately depicting flowerheads and an armorial device of a chevron between three roses. The bowl is also relief-cast in eight panels THOUGH WINE BE GOOD TOO MUCH OF THAT WIL MAKE ONE LEAN THOGH HE BE FATT. The foot with four roundels, one enclosing the arms of the City of London and another those of the Pewterers' Company. Trace of a touch-mark on the foot.
6in high (150mm)
British Museum, MLA 1980,5–2,1

This is one of a small number of extant examples of long-stemmed footed cups with relief-cast decoration.

107 BROAD-RIMMED CHARGER, c1660

A charger engraved all over with wriggle-work. In the well are the arms of the Butchers' Company of London and Exeter and the name Sarah Cox. On the rim the inscription PRESERVE THE TRUTH FALSEHOOD DEFIE WITH HONNESTIE STILL LIVE AND DIE and dated 'Anno Domini 1664'. By 'SB' with hallmarks.
18¼in diam (465mm)
Museum of London, 79.440

LIT. *Museum of London (1983), p16.*

106

107

108

109

108 DISH, late 17th century
A multiple-reeded dish decorated with a wrigglework tulip and two carnations and the date 1693. By Sir John Fryer. Several former owners' initials, including 'RW over D over IA' and the wriggled initials 'WD'. Four hallmarks on the rim.
16½in diam (420mm)
Private collection

This is the only known plate by Fryer. He was the son of a Buckinghamshire farmer. Brought to London in 1685 and apprenticed to Mr Harford of Bishopsgate Street, pewterer, Fryer suffered a hard apprenticeship which he recounted in his diary (now preserved as Guildhall Library MS 12017). Fryer reveals that a young master had to work very hard and commonly 'continued to take in work from other men, which in that business is called Trucking, but properly it is working of Journey work to other men' in the hope of building up a business of their own. Fryer was able to set up his own business immediately after gaining his freedom in 1692 thanks to financial support from his family. This was an unusual and fortunate head-start at this period. Elected a member of the Livery on 15 June 1696, Fryer was Master of the Company in 1710 and 1715, Alderman in 1709 and Lord Mayor 1720–1. (Hatcher and Barker, pp190–2, 247).

109 LOVING CUP, c1702
A cup with two beaded handles and wrythen lower body. The cup is cast decorated with GOD SAVE QUEEN ANNE on one side and the arms of the Pewterers' Company on the other. There are three ownership initials and a scratch date of 1702 on the underside. The touchmark 'IL' is repeated three times on the neck.
4¾ in high (124mm)
The Worshipful Company of Pewterers, 381

EXHIB. *Reading Museum, no. 144;* 'PEWTERWARE WITH ROYAL ASSOCIATIONS', *Pewterers' Hall, London, 1974, no. 35.*

LIT. *Pewterers' Company (1968/79); Michaelis (1969), p54.*

DECORATION

Most British pewter is relatively simple in design and is generally free of embellishments. Several methods of decoration were nevertheless popular and examples of each of the main forms are on display.

LIT. R.F. Michaelis, Decoration on English Pewterware, ANTIQUE COLLECTOR, October 1963 and February, August and December 1964; Hornsby (1983), for detailed discussion of all forms of pewter decoration.

CAST DECORATION

Under the influence of Italian silversmiths, there was a vogue for elaborately cast decorated pewter in Europe in the late 16th century. Finely cast intricate designs can be found on flagons, tankards, bowls and ewers of the period. Some of the most outstanding work was undertaken by François Briot (Lyons) and Caspar Enderlein (Nuremberg) but the technique, which required a high degree of skill both from the mould maker and the pewterer, was used in Germany, the Low Countries, France, Switzerland and Scandinavia. The earliest English examples, which lack some of the crisp detail found in Continental work, date from the late 16th century.

110

110   SAUCER OR PATEN, c1600
Cast decorated small plate with stylized flowers and foliage round the rim and with an inner band of leaves, together with a central cast boss.
5¼in diam (133mm)
Museum of London, A2704

Excavated from Norton Folgate, London.

LIT. Michaelis (1955), fig. 86; Michaelis (1969), p40; Museum of London (1983), p22.

111   WINE CUP, c1570–1610
A fine cast decorated wine cup with 'U' shaped bowl, baluster stem and stepped foot. The bands of decoration are composed of roses, marigolds and acorns. Made by 'IK' whose worn touch is on the foot in a heart and flowers mark.
7½in high (190mm)
The Worshipful Company of Pewterers, S2/211

LIT. Pewterers' Company (1968/79).

111

112

112 BEAKER, c1610–12
A cast decorated beaker, with roundels enclosing marigolds, flowers and crowns and the Prince of Wales feathers.
5¾in high (146mm)
Principal private collection

Found in a well at Hurstbourne Tarrant, Hampshire.

LIT. *Hornsby (1983), no. 1022.*

Attributed to Henry, eldest son of James I. who was invested as Prince of Wales in 1610 and died 1612.

113 TAZZA, c1616–21
The round dish on trumpet stem, the top of the plate cast WHAT WE THAT HAVE NOT RECEIVED OF THE LORD, 1616 and THE GIFT OF THOMAS HARVYE IN ANNO DO 1621 MARCH 31.
8in diam (203mm)
Christchurch Cathedral, Oxford, on loan from St Mary's, Great Shefford, Berks.

EXHIB. *Reading Museum, 1969, no. 55.*

LIT. *Hornsby (1983), no. 29; Michaelis (1955), figs. 81A and 81B; Michaelis (1969), p38.*

The date 1616 has been found on two other cast decorated items but its significance, if any, is not known.

113

Detail of 113

114   PORRINGER AND COVER, c1690
A two-eared porringer and cover. The bowl
has two relief-cast busts of William and Mary
and the cover has a relief Tudor rose, a royal
crown and two further busts. The cockerel
and one ear are restorations.
5¼in diam of bowl (133mm)
The Worshipful Company of Pewterers,
S5/501.32

LIT. *Pewterers' Company* (1968/79).

115   LOVING CUP, c1700–10
A two-handled loving cup, the handles decorated with cast beading and the cup gadrooned in the lower part of the body. By William Hux, the touch dated 1700. Initials
'BRM' on the foot.
4½in high (107mm)
Principal private collection

115

114

116

118

PUNCHED AND REPOUSSÉ DECORATION

In the second half of the 16th century flatware was occasionally decorated with patterns created by stamping punches of various designs onto the surface. This style of decoration is derived from the leather workers' trade, where similar punches were used. Two, three or four punches have usually been applied around the rim of plates, dishes and chargers. This form of decoration remained in use until the end of the 17th century. Pewter was also decorated in relief using the hammer, known as repoussé. Similar techniques are seen on 16th and 17th century brassware and on silver.

116 SAUCER, 16th century
A saucer with central boss and with one band of punch decoration around the semi-broad rim.
5in diam (127mm)
Principal private collection

117 CHARGER, c1620
Punch decorated charger with three bands of punches struck on the rim, each band employing a different punch. Owners' initials 'RA' and 'EW' struck on rim.
18in diam (457mm)
Principal private collection

118 FLAT-LIDDED TANKARD, c1695
A tankard with chased acanthus leaf decoration at the foot and top of the drum; the cover decorated in wrigglework and with twin love-bird thumbpiece. Owner's initials 'DH' stamped on body and the date 1694 engraved on the front. Made by Peter Duffield of London.
7in high (178mm)
The Worshipful Company of Pewterers, 173

LIT. *Pewterers' Company (1968/79);*
Cotterell (1929), pl LXX1.

117

LINE ENGRAVING

Pewter was frequently engraved with coats-of-arms, armorial devices and with owners' names and initials, but straight line engraving was seldom employed on English pewter for purely decorative purposes.

119   DISH, c1500–50

Dish with sloping sides and central boss, the bowl engraved with geometric patterns. Initials 'MBM' punched on dish.
14½in diam (370mm)
Principal private collection

EXHIB. *Usher Gallery, Lincoln, 1962, no. 238; Reading Museum, 1969, no. 28.*

LIT. *R.F. Michaelis,* DECORATION ON ENGLISH PEWTERWARE, *Antique Collector, October 1963.*

120   PLATE, mid-17th century

A broad-rimmed plate with the arms of the Drake family. By Thomas Haward (father or son).
10in diam (253mm)
Principal private collection

LIT. *Hornsby (1983), no. 120.*

The crest is the *Golden Hind,* Sir Francis Drake's ship.

119

120

121 CHARGER, c1640–60
A large charger with broad rim and central boss. The rim decorated with groups of huntsmen chasing a deer, a rabbit, a stag and a hare. Touchmark 'WB' with a stag or horse.
28¼in diam (717mm)
Principal private collection

LIT. *J. Pewter Soc., Spring 1985.*

121

WRIGGLEWORK

The form of engraving which was popular on pewter is known as wrigglework, which consists of a series of broken cuts across the surface, rather than a continuous line. Various tools may have been employed: a sharp implement such as a chisel struck with a hammer, or a burin. The designs were drawn and executed within the pewterers' workshops — they are simple and naive, many are religious or political. The earliest wrigglework dates from the 1650s and it was at its most popular between 1680 and 1725.

122   TAZZA, c1670
A tazza or footed plate with wrigglework decoration. The octagonal base has fruit and flower wriggling, and the plate is similarly engraved.
8½in diam (216mm)
Principal private collection

LIT. *Hornsby (1983), no. 363.*

123   BROAD-RIMMED DISH, c1650–60
A rare dish with wrigglework decoration depicting a dragon, its wings upraised within a wreath and dated 1656. The rim has leafy sprays between the sun and two planets inscribed 'Sovl, Ivprte Marsse'. On the rim is an inscription DAVID GUY AND HANNAH HIS WIFE LIVEING IN ELY TRINITY CORDWAINER COUSSIN TO GREAT GUY EARLE OF WARWICK.
16in diam (405mm)
British Museum, MLA 1983, 5–3, 1

One of the Earl of Warwick's supposed exploits was the killing of a dragon. David and Hannah Guy were married in 1645. The couple are presumably claiming direct descent from an illustrious ancestor. One of the earliest examples of wrigglework.

122

123

Detail of 123

124

125

124 FLAT-LIDDED TANKARD, c1670–80
With palm-tree thumbpiece, the body decorated with birds and tulips. By 'LA'.
6in high (152mm)
Principal private collection

EXHIB. *Usher Gallery, Lincoln, 1962, no. 160.*

125 FLAT-LIDDED TANKARD, c1680
With unusual thumbpiece, the body decorated with tulips, flowers and birds, initials 'MR' on lid. By Peter Duffield.
5in high (127mm)
Principal private collection

EXHIB. *Usher Gallery, Lincoln, 1962, no. 185.*

LIT. H.J.L.J. *Massé,* CHATS ON OLD PEWTER, *(rev) 1949, p27; Michaelis (1955), fig. 75.*

126 BROAD-RIMMED PLATE, c1661

A fine broad-rimmed wriggled plate, one of a
pair, with swan decoration. This example is
inscribed IN GOD IS ALL MY TRUST. The plate is
dated 1661. Former owners' initials 'RPE'
and 'BHA' stamped on the back. The touchmark of a crown over a rose with sun's rays
has the initials 'TB'.
8⅞ in diam (225mm)
*The Worshipful Company of Pewterers, S1/
123*

LIT. *H.H. Cotterell,* PEWTER DOWN THE AGES,
1932, p128; Cotterell, Riff and Vetter,
NATIONAL TYPES OF OLD PEWTER, *(rev) 1972,
p22; Peal (1983), p19; Pewterers' Company
(1968/79)*

One of the earliest examples of wrigglework,
the swan represents pure intelligence and
the word of God in Christian symbolism.

127 BATTLE OF WORCESTER PLATE, c1685

Wrigglework plate with triple-reeded rim.
The back of the plate has the name ROBART
wriggled on it. Made by 'LG', the mark with
barley sheaf, dated 1682. The hallmarks of
the marker are on the rim together with former owners' initials 'WRM'.
11in diam (280mm)
Frank Holt Collection

EXHIB. *Usher Gallery, Lincoln, 1962, no.
250; Reading Museum, 1969, no. 110.*

The decoration commemorates the Battle of
Worcester in 1651 when Charles II escaped
by hiding in an oak tree. The Boscobel Oak
theme is rare in pewter, but it also occurs on
slipware pottery (for example made by the
Toft family) and on needlework of this
period.

126

127

128

128 RESTORATION CHARGER, c1662
A wrigglework charger with the Stuart arms and portraits of Charles II and his Queen, and inscribed DIEU ET MON DROIT and VIVAT REX CAROLUS SECONDUS BEATI PACIFICUS 1662. With portcullis maker's touch.
22in diam (560mm)
Principal private collection

129 ENGRAVED CHARGER, c1660–65
Charger with the Stuart arms and the motto 'DIEU ET MON DROIT'. Initials 'HTM' struck on dish. With worn touchmark.
18½in diam (470mm)
Principal private collection

LIT. R.F. Michaelis, ROYAL OCCASIONS, *Antique Collector, August 1966, for details of 'Restoration chargers'.*

Charger with the Stuart arms and the motto 'DIEU ET MON DROIT'. Initials 'HTM' struck on dish. With worn touchmark.
18½in diam (470mm)

130   PLATE, c1690
An unusual wrigglework plate with a crowned lion motif. Former owners' initials 'FI' and 'AI' struck on rim. By Edward Gregory of Bristol, who died in 1696.
8¼in diam (210mm)
Principal private collection

LIT. Hornsby (1981), fig. 26; Hornsby (1983), no. 56.

In religious symbolism the lion represents God (and Judah), but this rather naive little beast may have been a reference to the continuation of the monarchy.

131   BEAKER, c1689-94
A wrigglework beaker of slightly tapering form with portraits of William and Mary. By John Kenton of London.
5¼in high (133mm)
Principal private collection

132   PLATE, c1680–1720
A wrigglework plate by Hutchins of Tavistock, engraved with birds and flowers. Owners' initials 'IGM'.
8¼in diam (210mm)
Principal private collection

130

132

131

133

PEWTER WITH ENAM ELLED MEDALLIONS

There are a few examples of pewter which have applied enamelled copper alloy medallions or badges. Dishes and chargers, which may well have been used with ewers at the dinner table or altar, are the most frequently found items which incorporate enamels. Usually referred to as 'Surrey enamels', all are either royal coats-of-arms or royal badges, mostly from the period of James I or Charles I. There is no evidence that such badges were made in Surrey, although there was a thriving brass works at Esher in the 17th century. Enamel work is also found on candlesticks and fire dogs or andirons of the late 17th century. Many of the enamel-mounted pewter dishes were made in Scotland and it is also likely that such work was being undertaken in London and elsewhere.

LIT. J. Pewter Soc., Autumn 1982, for an examination of pewter with such medallions.

133   PLATE, c1590–1600
A plate with 'Surrey' enamel. The royal arms are of the pre-Stuart form, used up to 1603. The touchmark 'WC' with half a sun and eight rays may be that of William Curtis.
9¾in diam (247mm)
The Worshipful Company of Pewterers, S1/102

LIT. Pewterers' Company (1968/79).

134   ENAMELLED EWER, c1610
An important jug with spout. An enamel boss with Stuart arms acts as a thumbpiece.
9½in high (242mm)
Ludlow Museum, SHRCM:H01937

EXHIB. Reading Museum, 1969, no. 57; PEWTER WITH ROYAL ASSOCIATIONS, Pewterers' Hall, London, 1974, no. 16.

Probably used with a bowl for washing hands at table.

134

135 ROSEWATER BOWL OR ALMS DISH, c1610–30
The dish has two rows of prunts, perles or flutes struck onto the rim and in the well. The central copper alloy enamel bears the arms of Charles I, supported by the initials 'CR'.
17¾in diam (452mm)
Principal private collection

LIT. *Hornsby (1983), no. 80.*

135

Detail of 135

137

RELIGIOUS OR CHURCH PEWTER

The Council of Westminster established in 1175 that pewter could only be used for sepulchral purposes — that is to provide a chalice or other object to be buried with a priest. It may be that many churches continued to provide pewter chalices in contravention of this because silver was too costly. However pewter was permitted for certain utensils. See for example nos. 136–139. The Church of England in 1603 permitted the use of 'a clean or sweet standing pot or stoup of pewter if not of purer metal'. From that date churches throughout England purchased communion flagons in considerable numbers. Pewter chalices and patens were also widely employed.

136   CRUET, 14th century
A six-sided vessel for wine or water, with relief-cast representations of God, the Virgin Mary and several saints. Made in thirteen separate parts: twelve cast-decorated panels form the body and the base is inserted.
5in high (128mm)
City Museum and Art Gallery, Birmingham

Excavated from Weoley Castle, near Birmingham.

EXHIB. *Reading Museum, 1969, no. 4.*

LIT. A. *Oswald,* TRANS., BIRMINGHAM AND WARWICKSHIRE ARCHAEOL. SOC., *vol 78, 1962, pp61ff; Brownsword and Simons, vol 93, forthcoming for an analysis of Weoley Castle and Ludlow cruets.*

The authors indicate that the cruet has a 99.9% tin content. The similar Ludlow cruet revealed a 99% tin content. These are unusual results when compared with other data for medieval pewter. Unfortunately comparative material (and analytical data) are not available to indicate place of manufacture, other than the main producing centre, London.

137   CRUET, 14th century
A small once spouted bulbous jug on lion feet.
4in high (100mm)
Chertsey Museum D791

From the Abbey river, Chertsey.

LIT. *SURREY ARCHAEOLOGICAL COLLECTIONS, vol 71, 1977.*

Examples of medieval 'round pots' are few. The 13th century cruet from White Castle, Wales, and now in the the National Museum of Wales, and a 15th century lidded baluster measure from the Thames (now in private hands) are the two other examples known.

Detail of 136

136

138 CHRISMATORY, 14th century
With three circular containers, two with lids
with attached hooks to lift the tow on which
the oil was administered. Standing on lion
feet (one a replacement). Fragmentary
'pitched roof' lid.
6¼in long (160mm)
*Christchurch Cathedral, Oxford, on loan
from the Rector and Churchwardens of St
John the Baptist, Granborough, Bucks*

Found in the wall of Granborough Church,
Bucks in 1880, almost certainly hidden in or
before 1552, the year of the second prayer
book of Edward VI, when church contents
with Romish origins were being destroyed.

LIT. *J. Pewter Soc., Autumn 1976; C.K.
Watson 'Remarks on the Granborough and
Canterbury Chrismatories'*, PROC.SOC. OF
ANTIQ. LONDON, 2nd series viii, 1879–81,
pp430–2.

A chrismatory was a container for holy oils
used in the Sacraments: *oleum infirmorum,
oleum sanctum* and chrisma. This is the only
known pre-Reformation chrismatory of pewter to survive.

138

139 LID OF PYX, 14th century
Hinged lid from an hexagonal pyx. One
side has a scene of the Annunciation,
with the Virgin and the Archangel, inscribed in relief in Lombardic script
+:AVE:MARIA:GRACIA:PLENA:DOMINUS:TECVM
(Hail Mary, full of grace, the Lord is with
thee). The other side has the Coronation of
the Virgin and the arms of England and
France flanking an oval setting, perhaps for
a crystal.
3⅛in high (79mm)
Museum of London, 86.202/1

Found at Bull Wharf, City of London.

A pyx is a small vessel in which the sacra-
ment is kept for future use.

139

141

142

140

140 PILGRIM AMPULLA, late 13th century
In the form of a shrine to St Thomas Becket of Canterbury, with scenes of his martyrdom on one side and of the penance of Henry II on the other; on one end St Thomas enthroned and on the other the Crucifixion.
2⅛in high (55mm)
Museum of London, 8779

From the Steelyard, Upper Thames Street, City of London, headquarters of the Hanseatic merchants.

EXHIB. AGE OF CHIVALRY, Royal Academy of Arts, London, 1987, no. 52.

LIT. B. Spencer, 'Pilgrim Souvenirs', p221 in catalogue of above exhibition, (eds) J. Alexander and P. Binski.

141 PILGRIM BADGE, c1350–1400
Virgin and Child. Openwork badge with enthroned figure of Virgin and Child beneath a canopy flanked by Edward the Confessor and St. Thomas Becket; below is the supporting figure of an angel. Fitted with clips at the sides to hold a coloured paper backing to set off the openwork.
5¼in high (135mm)
Museum of London, 84.394 and BWB 83–201

Found at Billingsgate, City of London, from two different sites.

EXHIB. AGE OF CHIVALRY, Royal Academy of Arts, London, 1987, no. 65.

LIT. B. Spencer, 'Pilgrim Souvenirs', p222 in catalogue of above exhibition, (eds) J. Alexander and P. Binski.

Probably a Canterbury badge representing Our Lady Undercroft. The fragments probably from different badges cast in the same mould.

142 PILGRIM BADGE, late 15th century
Figure of a priest in a pulpit flanked with angels, with a boot below a canopy. Inscribed 'MA 10 SCOR' for Magister Johannes Schorn.
2in high (50mm)
Museum of London, 8774

From the Thames foreshore, Queenhithe, City of London.

LIT. B. Spencer, 'King Henry of Windsor and The London Pilgrim', in J. Bird, H. Chapman and J. Clark (eds), COLLECTANEA LONDINIENSIA, (London and Middlesex Archaeol. Soc. Special Paper No 2, 1978) pp248–9 and 257–9.

John Schorn was rector of North Marston, Buckingham, in 1290. Stories grew about the miracles this pious man performed; on one occasion he 'conjured the devil into a boot'. In 1478 the Dean of Windsor obtained licence to move his shrine from North Marston to St. George's Chapel, Windsor Castle; this badge presumably comes from Windsor. North Marston is in the same ministry as Granborough (see cat. no.138)

143 PATEN, c1620–30
A Charles I paten with engraved symbol of ever-lasting life on the rim.
5¼in diam (133mm)
Principal private collection

144 FLAGON, c1622
A typical 'James I' flagon inscribed 'The Church flagon of Drayton 1622'. Worn touchmark on handle; initials 'WD' on erect thumbpiece.
14in high (355mm)
Principal private collection

145 PAIR OF CHURCH FLAGONS, c1685
A pair of 'beefeater' style church flagons with stepped lids and triple-cusp thumbpieces. Inscribed in three lines of script around the drum 'John Frankes Minister. Thomas Bennett Thomas Bennett Churchwardens 1685'. Made by Samuel Billings of Coventry.
12in high (305mm)
Frank Holt Collection

LIT. *J. Pewter Soc., Spring 1979; Hornsby (1983), no. 134.*

John Frankes was a graduate of Cambridge and was vicar of Queniborough in Leicestershire from 1680. There is a reference to the flagons in the parish accounts for 1685. The Bennetts, probably father and son, were members of one of the leading local families. Samuel Billings was a noted pewterer, and was Mayor of Coventry 1704–5.

144

143

145

146

146   CHALICE, mid-17th century

A chalice with small bowl, angular knop and wide base engraved with a cross.
5½in high (140mm)
Principal private collection

147   CHALICE OR WINE CUP, mid-17th century

A tulip-shaped cup or chalice with baluster stem. An unidentified touchmark 'TB' is struck beneath the base.
6¼in high (160mm)
The Worshipful Company of Pewterers, S2/208

LIT. Pewterers' Company (1968/79)

It is sometimes difficult to identify chalices used for Communion from wine cups employed domestically. Most chalices appear to have either a religious symbol or inscription and others, in the possession of a church, can be assumed to be ecclesiastical. Further examples may well have been domestic.

148   CHALICE OR WINE CUP, mid-17th century

A cup or chalice with small 'U' shaped bowl and baluster knopped stem, on stepped foot.
6½in high (162mm)
The Worshipful Company of Pewterers, S2/209

LIT. Pewterers' Company (1968/79).

148   147

149   CHALICE, c1680
A chalice with deep bowl and multiple ball
knopped stem.
6½in high (164mm)
Principal private collection

150   PASSOVER PLATE, c1680
A dish by Samuel Hancock of Pall Mall, London. The wrigglework decoration has two
rampant lions, a stag and flowers and, in
Hebrew, the names 'Zeligmann' and 'Yetta'
with the order of the Passover service around
the rim.
15in diam (382mm)
Jewish Museum, JM 1978, 1–7, 1

LIT. *Jewish Museum, Annual Report, 1981.*

As far as is known this is the only example of
an English pewter plate engraved with an
Hebraic inscription, though it is not known
for certain when or where the decoration was
executed. Passover plates, often with inscriptions, were popular in Germany and
other parts of central Europe from the 17th
to 19th centuries.
    The festival of the Passover usually takes
place in April and lasts for eight days. At a
symbolic feast (Seder) the Haggadah is read,
telling the story of the Israelites' deliverance
from bondage in Egypt. A special dish is used
to hold the unleavened bread, bitter herbs
and other food eaten at the meal or referred
to in the service.

149

150

SETTINGS

Three settings have been created to give visitors an idea of the way pewter was manufactured, sold and used in the home, in the late 17th century.

THE WORKSHOP

The workshop would have been a hot, dusty and dirty place. It was dominated by the pewterer's wheel and by a hearth or furnace where the ingots of tin, copper and lead were melted before casting. Moulds were stored on shelves or piled on the floor; the room was littered with tools. Pewterers frequently made bulk castings of parts such as handles and lids; these and other unfinished parts are kept ready for future use, together with examples of incomplete work which has been partly cleaned after casting to remove the surplus metal. (*Mould, tools and partly worked pewter, courtesy of James Yates Pewter of Twickenham*).

In the workshop is a selection of early 18th century tools, formerly used by the Townsend and Compton families (*on loan from The Worshipful Company of Pewterers*). These include a grater, spear burnisher, three turning hooks, two hawksbill burnishers, spade burnisher, a burnisher, two bouge hammers and a planishing hammer.

RETAIL SHOPS

Pewterers' shops of the period consisted of counter and storage areas, as represented in contemporary prints and drawings. Each shop would have been different. In some, most of the pewter might have been on open display, whilst in others the stock might have been kept wrapped or in the workshop, with only a small proportion put on view. In this shop a few items stand on open display, whilst other plates and dishes, baluster measures, candlesticks, salts and spoons are carefully wrapped in rag or oiled paper to prevent them getting dirty or oxidising. On the counter might be objects which the last customer had examined and scales – for pewter items were either sold by weight (as with plates and dishes) or individually priced. In front of the counter stand wicker baskets, used for transporting pewter to market, other shops, or for delivery to private clients. For longer journeys, especially by water, such as export to Europe or the American colonies, coopered barrels were used; one is in the process of being packed.
Pewter by Englefields, London

A HALL OR DINING ROOM

Whilst pewter had become widely popular at all levels of society by 1680, most homes would also have used leather, horn, wood, pottery and some brass or bronze objects for eating and serving at table. Between meals pewter would have been kept on a dresser or buffet or stored in a cupboard. A typical presentation of vessels is shown. People still used their personal knife and spoon, while forks were only just becoming popular. Home-brewed ale or beer was drunk from mugs made from pewter and other leading materials. A salt and candlestick are also placed on the table. Salt, important both for flavouring food at table and for preserving meat and fish, was costly and offered in small quantities.

Pewter was subject to heavy wear. Knife cuts and scratches soon accumulated and cleaning with grasses, sand or other rough abrasives, further damaged or dulled the surface. In regular use pewter soon lost its original sheen.

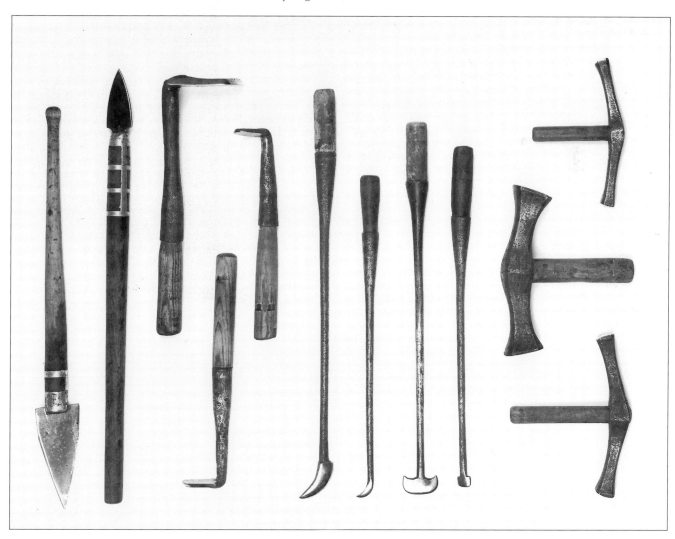

Suggested Further Reading

J. Hatcher and T.C. Barker, *A History of British Pewter*, 1974

R.F. Homer and D. Hall, *Provincial Pewterers*, 1985

P.R.G. Hornsby, *Pewter of the Western World*, 1983

Christopher Peal, *Pewter of Great Britain*, 1983

FOR MARKS

H.H. Cotterell, *Old Pewter its Makers and Marks*, 1929

C.A. Peal, *More Pewter Marks*, 1976, with Addenda, 1977.

The Pewter Society

The Pewter Society was founded in 1918 as the Society of Pewter Collectors and is the oldest society devoted to a specialised field of antiques. Its objectives are the study and understanding of old pewter, its documentation, restoration and preservation, and the history of its manufacture. A number of members have loaned pieces to this exhibition from their collections and have contributed to the text of the catalogue.

The Society has an extensive library, publishes a Journal and a Newsletter, and meets four times a year. Details of membership may be obtained from the Honorary Secretary, Dr. J.F. Richardson, Hunter's Lodge, Paddock Close, St Mary Platt, Sevenoaks, Kent, TN15 8NN.